DATE DUE			

*Culture and Customs
of Singapore and Malaysia*

**Recent Titles in
Culture and Customs of Asia**

Culture and Customs
of Singapore and Malaysia

WOODLAND HIGH SCHOOL
800 N. MOSELEY DRIVE
STOCKBRIDGE, GA 30281
(770) 389-2784

JAIME KOH AND STEPHANIE HO

Culture and Customs of Asia
Hanchao Lu, Series Editor

GREENWOOD PRESS
An Imprint of ABC-CLIO, LLC

A B C ⬥ C L I O

Santa Barbara, California • Denver, Colorado • Oxford, England

Library of Congress Cataloging-in-Publication Data
Koh, Jaime.
    Culture and customs of Singapore and Malaysia / Jaime Koh and Stephanie Ho.
        p. cm. — (Culture and customs of Asia)
    Includes bibliographical references and index.
    ISBN 978-0-313-35115-0 (hard copy : alk. paper) — ISBN 978-0-313-35116-7 (ebook)
    1. Ethnology—Singapore.   2. Ethnology—Malaysia.   3. Singapore—Social life and customs.   4. Malaysia—Social life and customs.   I. Ho, Stephanie.   II. Title.
    GN635.S55K64   2009
    305.80095957—dc22   2009015312

13   12   11   10   9   1   2   3   4   5

This book is also available on the World Wide Web as an eBook.
Visit www.abc-clio.com for details.

ABC-CLIO, LLC
130 Cremona Drive, P.O. Box 1911
Santa Barbara, California 93116-1911

This book is printed on acid-free paper ∞

Manufactured in the United States of America

Contents

Series Foreword

Geographically, Asia encompasses the vast area from Suez, the Bosporus, and the Ural Mountains eastward to the Bering Sea and from this line southward to the Indonesian archipelago, an expanse that covers about 30 percent of our earth. Conventionally, and especially in so far as culture and customs are concerned, Asia refers primarily to the region east of Iran and south of Russia. This area can be divided in turn into subregions, commonly known as South, Southeast, and East Asia, which are the main focus of this series.

The United States has vast interests in this region. In the 20th century, the United States fought three major wars in Asia (namely the Pacific War of 1941–45, the Korean War of 1950–53, and the Vietnam War of 1965–75), and each had a profound impact on life and politics in America. Today, America's major trading partners are in Asia, and in the foreseeable future the weight of Asia in American life will inevitably increase, for in Asia lie our great allies as well as our toughest competitors in virtually all arenas of global interest. Domestically, the role of Asian immigrants is more visible than at any other time in our history. In spite of these connections with Asia, however, our knowledge about this crucial region is far from adequate. For various reasons, Asia remains for most of us a relatively unfamiliar, if not stereotypical or even mysterious, "Oriental" land.

There are compelling reasons for Americans to obtain some level of concrete knowledge about Asia. It is one of the world's richest reservoirs of culture and an ever-evolving museum of human heritage. Rhoads Murphy, a prominent Asianist, once pointed out that in the part of Asia east of Afghanistan and south of Russia alone lies half the world, "half of its people and far more than half of its historical experience, for these are the oldest living civilized traditions." Prior to the modern era, with limited interaction and mutual influence between the East and the West, Asian civilizations developed largely independent from the West. In modern times, however, Asia and the West have come not only into close contact but also into frequent conflict: The result has been one of the most solemn and stirring dramas in world history. Today, integration and compromise are the trend in coping with cultural differences. The West—with some notable exceptions—has started to see Asian traditions not as something to fear but as something to be understood, appreciated, and even cherished. After all, Asian traditions are an indispensable part of the human legacy, a matter of global "commonwealth" that few of us can afford to ignore.

As a result of Asia's enormous economic development since World War II, we can no longer neglect the study of this vibrant region. Japan's "economic miracle" of postwar development is no longer unique, but in various degrees has been matched by the booming economy of many other Asian countries and regions. The rise of the four "mini dragons" (South Korea, Taiwan, Hong Kong, and Singapore) suggests that there may be a common Asian pattern of development. At the same time, each economy in Asia has followed its own particular trajectory. Clearly, China is the next giant on the scene. Sweeping changes in China in the last two decades have already dramatically altered the world's economic map. Furthermore, growth has also been dramatic in much of Southeast Asia. Today, war-devastated Vietnam shows great enthusiasm for joining the "club" of nations engaged in the world economy. And in South Asia, India, the world's largest democracy, is rediscovering its role as a champion of market capitalism. The economic development of Asia presents a challenge to Americans but also provides them with unprecedented opportunities. It is largely against this background that more and more people in the United States, in particular among the younger generation, have started to pursue careers dealing with Asia.

This series is designed to meet the need for knowledge of Asia among students and the general public. Each book is written in an accessible and lively style by an expert (or experts) in the field of Asian studies. Each book focuses on the culture and customs of a country or region. However, readers should be aware that culture is fluid, not always respecting national boundaries. While every nation seeks its own path to success and struggles to maintain its own identity, in the cultural domain mutual influence and integration among Asian nations are ubiquitous.

Each volume starts with an introduction to the land and the people of a nation or region and includes a brief history and an overview of the economy. This is followed by chapters dealing with a variety of topics that piece together a cultural panorama, such as thought, religion, ethics, literature and art, architecture and housing, cuisine, traditional dress, gender, courtship and marriage, festivals and leisure activities, music and dance, and social customs and lifestyle. In this series, we have chosen not to elaborate on elite life, ideology, or detailed questions of political structure and struggle, but instead to explore the world of common people, their sorrow and joy, their pattern of thinking, and their way of life. It is the culture and the customs of the majority of the people (rather than just the rich and powerful elite) that we seek to understand. Without such understanding, it will be difficult for all of us to live peacefully and fruitfully with each other in this increasingly interdependent world.

As the world shrinks, modern technologies have made all nations on earth "virtual" neighbors. The expression "global village" not only reveals the nature and the scope of the world in which we live but also, more importantly, highlights the serious need for mutual understanding of all peoples on our planet. If this series serves to help the reader obtain a better understanding of the "half of the world" that is Asia, the authors and I will be well rewarded.

Hanchao Lu
Georgia Institute of Technology

Preface

SINGAPORE AND MALAYSIA are two dynamic, independent countries located in Southeast Asia. Like siblings, the two are often mentioned in the same breath not only because of their close geographical proximity but also because of their shared history and culture. Singapore and Malaysia were historically regarded as part of the entity that was the Malay Archipelago, and the developments of both countries were closely intertwined until the independence of Singapore, in 1965. Despite the political separation, the two countries share a common cultural heritage, as is highlighted in this book. This is in no small part because of the similar ethnic composition of both countries, in which the Chinese, Malays, and Indians are the major ethnic groups. The main difference is the dominance of the Malays in Malaysia and the Chinese in Singapore.

The multiethnic, multireligious society in Singapore and Malaysia results in rich and diverse culture and customs. Although informed by tradition and history, culture and customs are nevertheless subject to the forces of globalization and modernization. The rapid pace of modernization in both countries resulting from the ambitions of their governments accelerates this process. Singapore has developed into a modern metropolis—from third world to first—in a matter of decades. Malaysia is also developing along a similar path with a vision of becoming a developed nation by the year 2020. In both countries, culture and custom are thus an intriguing blend of the old and the new, tradition and modernity.

This book adopts a thematic approach. In general, we emphasize the commonalities between culture and customs in Singapore and Malaysia, and the differences are highlighted through examples or in separate sections where necessary. Chapter 1 provides a general background to the land, people, economy, and history of Singapore and Malaysia. Chapter 2 introduces the major religions found in Singapore and Malaysia, as well as the concept of "Asian values," which ignited major international debates in the early 1990s. Following that, we highlight Singapore and Malaysia's traditional and contemporary literature and arts and crafts in Chapters 3 and 4, before discussing the architecture and housing in both countries in Chapter 5. Chapter 6 introduces the varied cuisines of the countries, and Chapter 7 discusses the issues of gender, courtship, and marriage. The colorful and packed festive calendar of Singapore and Malaysia is introduced in Chapter 8. We conclude the book with a look at a few key features of the lifestyles of Singaporeans and Malaysians.

The writing of this book has been an exciting journey, which has taken us from libraries and archives to numerous real-life encounters with Singaporeans and Malaysians. It has given us opportunities to travel, study, and re-examine the places that are so familiar to us so that we can share them with you. We are indebted to our editors, Professor Hanchao Lu and Kaitlin Ciarmiello, for their support and feedback, and to our family, friends, and all who have helped us along the way.

Chronology

68–550	Parts of the Malay Peninsula under the influence of the Funan empire.
600–1000	West coast of the Malay Peninsula under the influence of the Kingdom of Srivijaya.
1300–1400	Areas of the Straits of Malacca under the influence of the Kingdom of Majapahit circa 1300; Sang Nila Utama founds Temasek.
1396	Parameswara establishes the Malacca Sultanate.
1511	Portuguese capture Malacca.
1530s	Johor Sultanate established.
1641	Dutch capture city of Malacca from the Portuguese.
1786	Sultan of Kedah cedes island of Penang to the British, Sir Francis Light appointed as first superintendent of Penang.
1819	Sir Thomas Stamford Raffles establishes trading post on the island of Singapore.
1824	British and Dutch sign Anglo-Dutch Treaty (Treaty of London) delineating spheres of influence on the Malay Peninsula.

1826	British Straits Settlements, comprising Penang, Malacca, and Singapore, are formed; Britain and Siam sign Burney Treaty, limiting Siamese influence on Malay Peninsula.
1831–1832	Naning War in Malacca.
1832	Singapore replaces Penang as the capital of the Straits Settlements.
1841	Brunei confers title of rajah of Sarawak on James Brooke.
1846	Brunei cedes Sarawak to James Brooke.
1865	Charles Lee Moses acquires North Borneo.
1874	Residential System established in Malaya as a result of Pangkor Treaty.
1877	Baron von Overbeck receives full suzerainty of North Borneo from Brunei.
1881	British North Borneo Company buys rights to North Borneo.
1885	Anglo-Johor Treaty recognizes Sultan Abu Bakar as Sultan of Johor.
1888	Sarawak and North Borneo (Sabah) become British protectorates.
1896	Federated Malay States (Selangor, Perak, Negeri Sembilan, and Pahang) are formed.
1909	Britain and Siam sign the Anglo-Siamese Treaty, transferring the northern Malay states from Thai to British control.
1914	Johor receives British Adviser.
June 28, 1924	Opening of the Johor-Singapore Causeway.
December 8, 1941	Japanese troops land on Kota Bahru, Kelantan.
February 15, 1942	British surrender to Japanese in Singapore.
1942–1945	Japanese troops occupy Malaya and Singapore.
1945	Japanese troops in Malaya and Dutch East Indies officially surrender to British in Singapore on September 12; British Military Administration established in Malaya and Singapore.
1946	Singapore, Sarawak, and Sabah become Crown Colonies; Malayan Union is formed; United Malays National Organization and Malayan Indian Congress are established.

1948	Federation of Malaya replaces Malaya Union; first legislative council elections held in Singapore; State of emergency declared in Malaya.
1949	University of Malaya in Singapore is formed (merger of King Edward VII College of Medicine and Raffles College).
December 1, 1950	Maria Hertogh riots in Singapore.
September 22, 1951	Singapore proclaimed a city by Royal Charter.
1954	People's Action Party is formed.
1955	Rendel Constitution; Baling Peace Talks are held between British and Malayan authorities and the Communist Party of Malaya; David Marshall elected first chief minister of Singapore; Hock Lee Bus riots; general elections held in Malaya; Nantah University, the first Chinese university in Singapore, is formed.
1956	Independence talks for Malaya begin in London.
1957	Malaya achieves independence from Britain on August 31; Tunku Abdul Rahman becomes first prime minster of Federation of Malaya; Malaya admitted to the United Nations on September 17.
1959	Singapore attains self-government; Yusof bin Ishak sworn in as Singapore's first Yang di-Pertuan Negara (president) and Lee Kuan Yew becomes the first prime minister of Singapore.
1961	Tunku Abdul Rahman proposes formation of Malaysia, comprising the Federation of Malaya, Singapore, Sarawak, Sabah, and Brunei.
1962	University of Malaya Kuala Lumpur campus re-established as University of Malaya; Singapore campus becomes University of Singapore.
1963	Singapore conducts referendum on joining Malaysia; Malaysia, comprising Malaya, Singapore, Sabah, and Sarawak, is formed; Indonesia launches Konfrontasi against Malaysia; Operation Coldstore—arrest of 113 prominent pro-Communists and unionists in Singapore; TV Singapura commences first broadcast; Television Malaysia launched in Kuala Lumpur.
July 21, 1964	Race riots in Singapore.
1964	Malaysian Solidarity Convention established.

August 9, 1965   Singapore expelled from Malaysia, gains independence.

September 21, 1965   Singapore admitted to the United Nations.

March 1967   National Service bill passed in Singapore, making conscription
                        compulsory for all males reaching 18 years of age; Association
                        of Southeast Asian Nations (ASEAN) formed.

May 13, 1969   Race riots in Malaysia following Alliance loss in general elec-
                        tions; Malaysia declares state of emergency.

1970   Tun Abdul Razak becomes second prime minister of Malaysia.

1971   British military withdraws from Singapore; Malaysia launches
                        the New Economic Policy.

1973   Barisan Nasional replaces Alliance as the ruling coalition in
                        Malaysia.

1976   Tun Hussein Onn becomes third prime minister of Malaysia.

1981   Mahathir Mohammad becomes the fourth prime minister of
                        Malaysia.

1989   Chin Peng signs peace treaty with Malaysia.

1990   Goh Chok Tong replaces Lee Kuan Yew as second prime min-
                        ister of Singapore.

2003   Mahathir Mohammad steps down as prime minister of Ma-
                        laysia; Abdullah Badawi takes over.

2004   Malaysia introduces National Service program for 17–18-
                        year-old Malaysians; Lee Hsien Loong becomes third prime
                        minister of Singapore.

2008   Malacca and George Town receive World Heritage listing by
                        UNESCO; Singapore wins bid to host inaugural 2010 Youth
                        Olympic Games; Singapore wins silver in women's table ten-
                        nis in Beijing Olympics.

April 2, 2009   Najib Abdul Razak sworn in as sixth prime minister of
                        Malaysia.

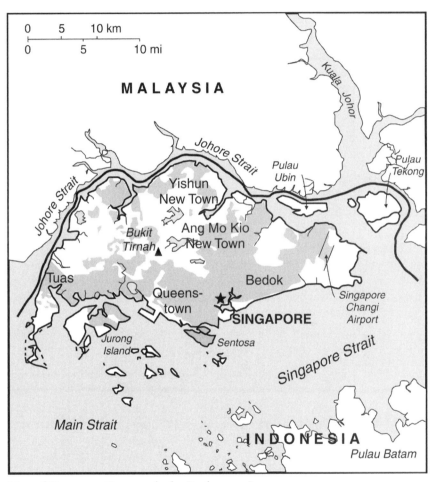

Map of Singapore. Cartography by Bookcomp, Inc.

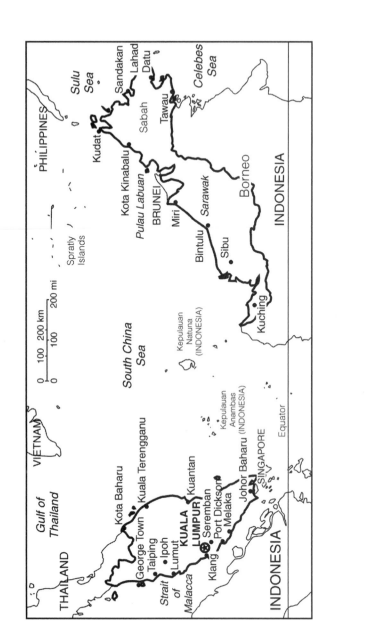

Map of Malaysia. Cartography by Bookcomp, Inc.

1

Land, People, and History

ALTHOUGH INDEPENDENT AND sovereign entities, Singapore and Malaysia, like two siblings in a family who have different personalities, are bound by a common geography, history, and culture. Despite the countries' tumultuous histories, occasional political tensions, and different paces of development, their interdependence and constant interaction are inevitable. Geographically, Singapore and Malaysia are adjacent. Historically, these two countries have been part of the same entity—the Malay Archipelago, British Malaya, and finally Malaysia—until as recently as 1965. Despite their political differences, there are many cultural similarities between the two countries, as the next few chapters will show. It is thus hardly surprising that Singapore and Malaysia are often regarded as one entity or are mentioned in the same breath.

LAND AND CLIMATE

Though the climate is undeniably a "hot one," the heat, tempered by alternating land and sea breezes, is seldom oppressive except just before rain, and the thermometer never attains anything approaching those torrid temperatures which are registered in . . . parts of the temperate zones. The rainfall is not excessive . . . and there is no regular rainy season. In fact it rains in moderation all the year round.[1]

Although written more than 130 years ago, this passage remains an apt description of the climate of Singapore and Malaysia. It is often said that the four seasons in Singapore and Malaysia are hot, hot, hot, and hot. The only variety is in the intensity of the heat and humidity. Located near the equator, Singapore and Malaysia experience high humidity (average 84.3%), high temperatures (average 80.2°F), and heavy rainfall (2,000 mm to 2,500 mm) throughout the year. Temperatures in Malaysia's highlands are cooler, ranging between 59°F and 77°F.

Singapore is an island state located between latitudes 1°09'N and 1°29'N and longitudes 103°36'E and 104°25'E. It is one of world's smallest nation states, with a land area of just 270 square miles. Much of the east and west coast of the main island has been reclaimed since the 1960s to increase the land area. Singapore's territories also include 63 offshore islands, the larger ones being Pulau Tekong and Pulau Ubin in the northeast and Sentosa, a tourist destination, to the south. With a population density of about 16,052 persons per square mile, Singapore ranks as one of the world's most densely populated countries. With the exception of designated industrial areas and a couple of nature reserves around the island, Singapore is a totally urban society, with a cityscape dominated by skyscrapers and modern buildings. Most of the rural areas were developed into suburban housing estates or industrial estates during the period of modernization in the 1970s and 1980s.

Malaysia, connected to Singapore by two causeways, is spread over 127,320 square miles between 2° and 7° north of the equator. It is a federation of 13 states—Johor, Kedah, Kelantan, Malacca, Negri Sembilan, Pahang, Perak, Perlis, Penang, Selangor, Terengganu, Sabah, and Sarawak—and three federal territories (Kuala Lumpur, Labuan, and Putrajaya). Of the 13 states, 11 are located on the peninsular mainland, while Sabah and Sarak are located on the island of Borneo, separated from the mainland by the South China Sea. These two states also share borders with the sultanate of Brunei and the Indonesian state of Kalimantan. Unlike the mainland, Sabah and Sarawak, which account for about 60 percent of Malaysia's total land area, have mountainous interiors and luxuriant rainforests and are thus ideal locations for eco- and adventure tourism. There are major cities in the various states, including the capital, Kuala Lumpur, and the new administrative center of Putrajaya, but a large part of the country remains rural.

PEOPLE

Multiculturalism is a feature of Singapore and Malaysian societies. There is little difference in the ethnic composition of both countries, with the major ethnic groups being Malays, Chinese, and Indians. There are, however, two important differences. The first is in the proportion of the total population that each ethnic group represents. Demographically, Singapore is a Chinese-dominated society, with the Chinese making up some 75.1 percent of Singapore's population of 4.3 million. The Chinese are followed by the Malays (13.7%), Indians (8.7%), and an aggregation of other ethnic groups—including Peranakans, Eurasians, Arabs, Armenians, Jews—nominally classified as "Others" (2.1%).[2] In Malaysia, the Malays are the majority, making up some 57 percent of Malaysia's estimated 27.7 million people.[3] The Chinese form the second largest ethnic group, accounting for 23.7 percent of the population. Indigenous groups make up 11 percent of the population, while Indians constitute 7.1 percent and "Others" 7.9 percent of the total. In Malaysia, the Malays, together with indigenous groups, are collectively known as the *bumiputera,* literally meaning "sons of the soil." It is an indication of their status and affords them preferential treatment. The *bumiputera* make up about 60 percent of Malaysia's population.[4]

The second demographic difference between the two countries is that Malaysia has a large number of indigenous tribal groups. There are at least 50 indigenous groups in Malaysia, most of which are found in the East Malaysian states of Sabah and Sarawak. One of the oldest indigenous groups on the Peninsula is the Orang Asli (aborigines), who are believed to have lived on the Peninsula as early as 25,000 years ago. The group is divided into 19 subgroups, which are identified by their ecological niches. Among East Malaysia's numerous colorful tribal groups are the renowned headhunting Iban, the Bidayuh, the Kadazan, the Melanau, the Kayan, the Kenyah, the Kajang, the Lyn Bawang, the Kelabit, the Bisaya, the Tagal, the Penan, and the Punan. Singapore, on the other hand, does not have a distinct indigenous group. When the British landed in Singapore in 1819, it was recorded that there were about 150 Orang Laut (Sea People), an indigenous group that lived throughout the Malay and Indonesian archipelagos. Many of the Malays in Singapore today are of mixed descent, their ancestors having intermarried with other groups, and they are regarded as the indigenous people under the Singapore constitution.

Although considered ethnic minorities in Singapore and Malaysia, the Peranakans and the Eurasians are unique to this region. Both groups trace their ancestry back to the 15th-century Malacca Sultanate. Colloquially, the Peranakans are also known as "Baba" (for the males) and "Nonya" (to refer to the females). Historically, they were also known as "King's Chinese," "Straits Chinese," or "Straits-born." The Peranakans are the offspring of Chinese traders who arrived in Malacca and married local Malay women, while the Eurasians are the direct offspring of Malacca's Portuguese conquerors who married local women. Today, the term "Eurasian" is generally used to refer to those who descended from intermarriages between Europeans and locals. Generally, the Peranakans are found mainly in the former Straits Settlements—Singapore, Penang, and Malacca—while the Eurasians are found mostly in Singapore and Malacca. Historically, the Peranakans and the Eurasians were among the prominent leaders and businessmen during colonial times. Today, many of them continue to play an important role in business and the cultural sectors.

An array of languages is spoken in Singapore and Malaysia. In addition to the main languages of English, Mandarin, Malay, and Tamil, there are also numerous Chinese and Indian dialects. In Singapore, English, Mandarin, Malay, and Tamil are designated as the four official languages. English was the colonial language and was retained as the lingua franca of government, business, and education. The dominance of English in Singapore was a rational decision: English was the international language of business, science, and technology and was thus essential for economic development. Furthermore, English serves as a relatively neutral language for interethnic communication. After independence, in 1965, English was made the main language of education, while the other languages—Mandarin, Malay, and Tamil—were taught as second languages, or mother tongues. Mandarin and Tamil were chosen as the "official" languages of the Chinese and Indian communities as they were considered to be more easily understood regardless of the dialect subdivisions within the communities. This language policy was part of the Singapore government's management of multiculturalism and multiracialism.

Malaysia, on the other hand, does not have a deliberate multilingual policy. Although various languages and dialects are spoken in Malaysia, Bahasa Melayu, or the Malay language, is the national language as stipulated by the Malaysian constitution. It is the language used for all official purposes and in all matters relating to the federal, state, and local governments, as well as by the public authorities. And, until 2002, Malay was the main medium of instruction in all state schools. As a result, regardless of race, almost all Malaysians are fluent in the language. In 2002, in an effort to increase the Malaysians' fluency in English, the Malaysian government announced that English was to be used as the main medium of instruction in mathematics (arithmetic) and science. In the past few years, many government agencies also began to introduce English versions of their Web sites, which had hitherto been available in Malay only.

ECONOMY

Trade has been the foundation of Singapore's economic development. From its precolonial days through its time as a British crown colony, the exchange of goods and services was key to Singapore's success. During the early 19th century, Singapore maintained a small agricultural economy with the industrial cultivation of cash crops such as gambier and vegetables. But agriculture was never as central to the island's economy as trade. Since independence, Singapore has embarked on a diversification of its economy. It sped up its industrialization program, developing specifically the manufacturing sector. At the same time, Singapore also began to develop other economic pillars, namely tourism, financial services, and building and construction, as well as the petrochemical and pharmaceutical industries. Today, Singapore is considered a regional hub for financial and business services in Asia, and many international corporations have established their headquarters here.

The Malaysian economy has a character totally different from Singapore's. Historically, the foundation of Malaysia's economy was its agricultural sector, which remains critical today. Commodities such as petroleum, palm oil, natural rubber, and timber continue to be prime movers of the Malaysian economy. But agricultural products now account for only 9 percent of Malaysia's annual gross domestic product, with manufacturing accounting for the largest portion, at 32 percent.[5] The other bases of the modern Malaysian economy are mining, food and beverage services, wholesale and retail trade, finance, real estate, and general business. During the premiership of Mahathir Mohammad (1981–2003), one of the major economic goals of Malaysia was to develop the country into one of the high-tech economic powers of Southeast Asia. The government, then, introduced *Vision 2020* (*Wawasan 2020*), an action plan to foster Malaysia's development into an industrialized country. Among the plan's objectives were to increase Malaysia's gross domestic product by about 7 percent per year, to privatize the economy, and to speed up the use of technology in business and government.[6]

GOVERNMENT

Politically, Singapore and Malaysia inherited the British Westminster parliamentary system. Since 1959, Singapore has been governed by a single political party—the People's Action Party (PAP). Although there have been opposition parties, they have been unable to challenge the PAP politically. The leader of the PAP holds the position of prime minister, the head of the Singapore government. The prime minister heads the Cabinet and the unicameral Parliament. Unlike the U.S. Cabinet, which functions largely as an advisory council to the head of government (the president), the Singapore Cabinet collectively decides the government's policies and has influence over legislation. The president is the head of state. The president was at first chosen by the Parliament and had largely ceremonial duties, but that has changed. In 1991, the constitution was amended to allow for election of the president to a six-year term. In addition to the ceremonial duties, the president now has limited veto power in several key areas, for example, the use of the national reserves and appointments to key judiciary positions.

The Singapore judiciary includes the Supreme Court and the subordinate courts, which hear civil and criminal cases. The system is based on the British common law system. The higher courts' decisions are binding on courts of equal or lower status within their jurisdiction. The judiciary is presided over by the chief justice, while the senior district judge has overall responsibility for the administration of the subordinate courts. The chief justice and the other judges of the Supreme Court are appointed by the president, acting on the advice of the prime minister.

The members of Parliament (MPs) are elected to office in elections that take place every four to five years. Political parties may field candidates in either single-member constituencies (SMCs) or group representation constituencies (GRCs), where teams of between three and six candidates compete. At least one candidate in the team must belong to a minority race. Responding to criticisms of a lack of opposition parties in Singapore, the government introduced two new types of MPs—nonconstituency members of Parliament (NCMPs) and nominated members of Parliaments (NMPs). The NCMPs are members of the opposition political parties who are not elected to power during an election but are appointed as MPs. NMPs, on the other hand, are not connected to any political parties but are appointed by the president for a two-and-a-half-year term. The main objectives of these appointments are to ensure that there is at least a minimum number of opposition members in Parliament so that a wide range of community views are represented. Both the NCMPs and the NMPs can fully participate in Parliament but have more limited powers than MPs. For example, they cannot vote on amendments to the constitution or the use of public funds. They also cannot participate in votes of no-confidence in the government or vote to remove the president from office.

Malaysia's political system is that of a federal parliamentary monarchy. Instead of a president, the Yang di-Pertuan Agong (the king) is the federal head of the state. The king is elected to a five-year term, and the post is rotated among the nine hereditary sultans of the Malay states. Penang, Malacca, Sabah, and Sarawak, which do have not hereditary rulers but only titular Governors, do not participate in the selection of the king. The prime minister is the head of the federal government and the leader of a multiparty system. Whereas Singapore has largely been a one-party state, dominated by the PAP, Malaysia's government is made up of a coalition, known as the Barisan Nasional (National Front). The coalition is made up of 14 political parties, of which the three largest are the United Malays National

Organization (UMNO), the Malaysian Chinese Association (MCA), and the Malaysian Indian Congress (MIC), which represent the three major races in Malaysia. There are numerous opposition parties in Malaysia, with the most prominent being the Democratic Action Party (DAP), the Pan-Malaysian Islamic Party (PAS), and the People's Justice Party (Keadilan).

The state governments are led by chief ministers who are selected by the various state assemblies to advise the sultans or the governors in governance matters. Malaysia has a bicameral parliament consisting of the lower house, the House of Representatives or Dewan Rakyat (Chamber of the People), and the upper house, the Senate or Dewan Negara (Chamber of the Nation). Parliamentary elections are held at least once every five years, and the federal Cabinet is chosen from among members of both houses of Parliament.

The judicial system is also based on that of the English common law. As in Singapore, the constitution sets out the legal framework of the country and the rights of the citizens. The judicial power rests in the federal court system, which is made up of the Federal Court, the Court of Appeal, the High Courts, and the Subordinate Courts. In addition to secular law—that is, civil and criminal law—the Malaysian legal system also has a secondary source of law, Islamic law, generally known as the Syariah law, which applies only to Muslims. The Syariah law is under the auspices of the Syariah Court, which has jurisdiction in civil matters involving Muslims.

HISTORY

There are several themes to consider when studying the history of Singapore and Malaysia. The first, and perhaps most significant, is the interconnectedness of the region's geography and history. Until the coming of the Europeans, there was little concept of boundaries in the territories now known as Singapore, Malaysia, and Indonesia. This region was often collectively referred to as the Malay Archipelago. The region is also at times referred to as Nusantara, an ancient geographical concept of the Malay world, encompassing the territories of Peninsular Malaysia, Singapore, most of the Indonesian islands, and the islands in the Philippine archipelago. Within Nusantara, ancient kingdoms and empires stretched across the region, as did their influences. The political and territorial boundaries of contemporary Singapore, Malaysia, Thailand, and Indonesia emerged only in the mid-20th century with the coming of the European colonial powers. Prior to this, territories were demarcated by the "spheres of influence" of the various ruling empires.

The growth and development of Singapore and Malaysia can be largely attributed to two related factors: geographic location and trade. The Malay Peninsula is accessible from both the Straits of Malacca and the Sunda

Straits and is well sheltered by the Indonesian archipelago. More important, it lay at the crossroads of the Europe-Asia trade route linking the industrializing Europe to the resource-rich China and Malay Archipelago. The geographic location, coupled with the Peninsula's abundant natural resources, was critical to the area's rise as the emporium of Southeast Asia. The importance of trade in the development of the Malay Peninsula cannot be overemphasized. It was the foundation on which the Malay sultanates were built and the reason that brought foreign powers—the Portuguese, the Dutch, and the British—to the region. It was also the motivating factor for power tussles over the control of the region.

Kingdoms and Empires

The 15th century is often regarded as the beginning of the history of modern Malaysia and the 19th century for modern Singapore. Historians have pointed to the difficulty of reconstructing the pre-15th-century history of the Malay Peninsula because of the lack of coherent written sources. The founding of the Malacca Sultanate and the subsequent arrival of the colonial powers inspired court writings, travel notes, and administrative documents that formed the bibliographical basis for the region's history. This does not mean, however, that there was no history before the 15th century. Archaeological evidence and references scattered among Chinese, Indian, and Arabic writings do provide clues to the region's history. Human relics discovered in Sarawak's Niah Caves date human beginnings in Southeast Asia back some 35,000 years. Various other excavations around the Malay Peninsula have also uncovered artifacts pointing to human activities way before the arrival of the Europeans. Excavations in Singapore have unearthed various artifacts, including ceramics, porcelain ware, Indian glass beads, and copper coins, pointing to the presence of some form of trading community on the island prior to the arrival of the British in the 19th century. Although their beginnings were ambiguous and hard to pinpoint, there are references to the Malay Peninsula and Singapore in various sources, although they are called by various names—Golden Chersonese, Nanyang (South Seas), Pu Luo Chung, and Temasek among others.

Until the 16th century, the Malay Peninsula was ruled by a succession of ancient kingdoms and empires, beginning with the Indochinese kingdom of Funan, followed by the Sumatran kingdom of Srivijaya. The Hindu-Malay Kingdom of Langkasutra and the Kingdom of Kedah existed at the same time and were established in the present state of Kedah. Langkasutra was at one point absorbed by the Funan Kingdom and later by Srivijaya. While Funan's influence extended only to the northern part of the Malay Peninsula, Srivijaya's influence extended to both sides of the Straits of Malacca and to the west coast of the Borneo island. The Javanese empire of Majapahit eventually filled the political vacuum left by Srivijaya, which claimed dominion over most of Sumatra and the Malay Peninsula.

The legacy of Srivijaya, however, survived through a Palembang prince, Parameswara, who first arrived in Temasek (present day Singapore) at the close of the 14th century. According to the *Sejarah Melayu,* a literary chronicle covering the 600-year span of the Malacca Sultanate, Temasek was "discovered" by a Palembang prince, Sri Tri Buna (also known as Sang Nila Utama), in the late 12th or early 13th century. Legend has it that he established a city on the island, naming it Singapura (Lion City) after sighting a mythical beast with a red body, black head, and white breast, "strong and active in build"—which he believed to be a lion. The *Sejarah Melayu* further records that "Singapura became a great city, to which foreigners resorted in great numbers so that the fame of the city and its greatness spread throughout the world."[7]

According to Portuguese accounts, Parameswara established himself as ruler of Temasek after ousting the local chiefs. There are differing accounts of Parameswara's eventual flight from Singapore. An account by the Portuguese writer, Tome Pires, records that the Siamese drove Parameswara out, while the *Sejarah Melayu* describes an attack by Majapahit troops from Java. In both stories, Parameswara is said to have set himself up in Malacca around 1396 after fleeing from Singapore. There, with protection from China's Ming Dynasty, he expanded the small fishing settlement into the formidable Malacca Sultanate, which became the nucleus of development of the Malay Peninsula. Malacca's influence and power grew throughout the 15th century. At the height of its powers, the Malaccan empire included much of the Peninsula: from Temasek and Johor in the south, to Kedah and Patani in the far north, as well as the east coast of Sumatra.

Coming of the Colonial Powers

By the mid-16th century, three main centers of power dominated the Malay Peninsula—Portuguese Malacca, Johor, and Aceh. The city of Malacca was at the center of the power struggles. The Portuguese first arrived in Malacca in 1509 on a trade mission, during which several of their members were arrested and imprisoned. They returned in 1511 and used the incident as a pretext to attack Malacca. They succeeded in conquering the city of Malacca, ending the dominance of the great Malacca Sultanate. One of the first tasks the Portuguese undertook was to build a fort, the A Famosa, which protected Malacca from numerous attacks from rival powers.

Malacca's ruler, Sultan Mahmud Shah, fled to the island of Bintan (part of Indonesia today), south of Singapore. Sultan Mahmud Shah never gave up the idea of recapturing Malacca from the Portuguese. From his new base, he launched several attacks on Portuguese Malacca, but all without much success. In 1526, the Portuguese counterattacked and destroyed the capital he had established at Bintan. Sultan Mahmud Shah fled to Sumatra and died there in 1528. He was succeeded by his younger son, Sultan Alauddin, who moved to Johor and eventually established the Johor Sultanate with its capital on the Johor River. Like his father, Sultan Alauddin attempted to retake Malacca from the Portuguese in the 1540s but failed. Meanwhile, Sultan Mahmud Shah's eldest son, who took the name Sultan Muzaffar Shah, established a new state in Perak in 1529.

The Dutch arrived in the Malay Peninsula as early as 1602 on a trading mission. Keen to control the lucrative spice trade from the Malay Archipelago, the Dutch established themselves in Batavia, Indonesia, which soon overtook Malacca as the trading center of the archipelago. The arrival of the Dutch coincided with the decline of the Portuguese, who had lost many of their regional trading outposts to the Dutch. The Dutch, however, were eyeing the prize catch—Malacca, which was then regarded as

the market of all India, of China, and the Moluccas, and of other islands round about, from all which places . . . arrive ships which come and go incessantly charged with an infinity of merchandises.[8]

In June 1641, the Portuguese capitulated to the Dutch attackers. Malacca fell to the Dutch, thus establishing a Dutch trade monopoly in the region that lasted for most of the 17th century.

During much of the 16th century, there was a constant power struggle involving Portuguese Malacca, Johor, and the rapidly rising power of Aceh, just across the Straits of Malacca. Aceh had on various occasions sought to capture Malacca from the Portuguese, although without much success. In 1575, Aceh captured the state of Perak, and, in the early years of the 17th century, extended its control over the states of Pahang and Kedah. But it failed to conquer Johor and was defeated in 1629 by the combined forces of Portuguese Malacca, Johor, and the Siamese state of Patani. Siam (Thailand) also sought to extend its influence in the Malay Peninsula during the 17th century. Its interest in the Peninsula began in the 13th century, and throughout the 14th and 15th centuries Siam sought to compete with the Malacca and Johor Sultanates in extending its hegemony over the Peninsula. Although it was not as successful as the European colonial powers in establishing itself in the Peninsula, Siam exerted varying degrees of control over several kingdoms in present-day southern Thailand and northern Malaysia until the early 20th century.

British Malaya

When the British arrived at the end of the 18th century, the Malay Peninsula was an assortment of politically divided states. To the north, the states

The 16th-century fort A Famosa, built by the Portuguese to defend the city of Malacca, still stands today, bearing witness to the rich history of the city. Courtesy of the author.

of Kedah, Kelantan, and Terengganu were under Siamese suzerainty. Perak and Selangor were independent states, Malacca was in Dutch hands, and the rest of the southern area of the Peninsula was part of the Johor Sultanate. The arrival of the British was especially significant, for it was during their period of influence that the boundaries of the countries we know today as Singapore, Malaysia, and Indonesia began to take shape. Interestingly, the British possessions in Malaya were established by trading companies and individuals, and not by the British government. Penang, Malacca, and Singapore were established as trading posts to facilitate British regional trade. Even subsequent expansion into the other Malay states was motivated primarily by the need to maintain stability and access to raw materials for economic purposes.

From the late 17th century, the British were increasingly pressured to secure a base east of the Bay of Bengal. There were two reasons for this. The first was to gain the upper hand in their rivalry with the French in India and mainland Southeast Asia. A base close to Southeast Asia would make it easier to protect the British possessions and to prevent the French from gaining a foothold. The second reason for a base on the eastern side of the Bay of Bengal was to ensure the safety of the India-China trade, which was growing in importance in the 18th century. Several missions were sent to scout the region for an appropriate site. The British initially wanted to establish a trading settlement on Borneo, given its proximity to southern China. But the site was later regarded as too far east to attract traders plying the Straits of Malacca. Furthermore, the area was pirate-infested. The British eventually abandoned the Borneo site.

In 1771, Sir Francis Light, a merchant captain of the British East India Company (EIC), arrived in Kedah to find the sultan keen to obtain European assistance in fending off potential invasions from Siam. Despite the imperative to secure a base, the EIC was reluctant to become caught up in the politics of the Malay states. Thus, Light's plan to secure a trading site in the Straits of Malacca was left to languish for the next 12 years as the British were preoccupied with political developments in Europe. The British changed their mind about Penang after successive failed attempts to locate a suitable site for their purposes. It was under such circumstances that Light managed to persuade the EIC directors to reconsider Penang. In 1786, the sultan of Kedah ceded the island to the British, marking the beginning of more than a century of British involvement on the Peninsula. Light, whose eldest son William Light was the founder of the Australian city of Adelaide, was appointed Penang's first superintendent.

The first superintendent of Penang, Sir Francis Light, at his final resting place in the Protestant Cemetery in Penang. Courtesy of the author.

By the end of the Napoleonic Wars, in 1815, the British had come to recognize the advantages the Malay Archipelago offered to the British interests. One man in particular, Thomas Stamford Raffles of the EIC, was keen to expand British influence in the region by establishing trading settlements. But the British government rebuffed Raffles' proposals, fearing that they might antagonize the Dutch, their ally against a potentially recalcitrant France in Europe, which already had significant territories in the region—Malacca and some of the Riau islands. But Raffles, then lieutenant general of Java, remained convinced that the British needed a base in the south of the Malay Peninsula, in the heart of the Dutch empire. While on a scouting mission to the southern part of the Malay Peninsula in search of a suitable base, Raffles landed at Singapore.

There is debate on whether the landing on Singapore was an accident or planned. But what is certain is that when Raffles landed on the island on January 28, 1819, Singapore was part of the Johor Sultanate under Sultan Abdul Rahman, who was under Dutch protection. Hence, although there was no Dutch presence on the island, it was indirectly under Dutch influence. Raffles, keen to secure the island for the British, circumvented the situation by recognizing Tengku Hussein, Sultan Abdul Rahman's elder brother, who had been bypassed for the Johor throne and was in exile in Riau, as the sultan of Johor. According to the account by Sir Richard Winstedt, a British administrator, Raffles was aware of the situation:

So aware that under Dutch surveillance neither Sultan 'Abdu'r-Rahman (*sic*) of Lingga nor the Undertaking at Riau would be able to convey any rights at Singapore to the British, Raffles determined to go back on the British recognition of the young brother . . . and to install . . . Tengku Hussain as the rightful Sultan of the old empire of Johore. . . . Raffles paid two Malay gentlemen $500 each to fetch the "rightful heir" from Riau. Tengku Hussain pretended he was going fishing and sailed on to Singapore, where . . . he was installed . . . as Sultan of Johor. Raffles gave him a thousand dollars and rolls of black and yellow cloth.[9]

Sultan Hussein was thus installed in Singapore on February 6, 1819. One of the key players in the founding of modern Singapore was the Temenggong, chief of the island. When Raffles first landed on the island to discuss the possibility of establishing a trading port there, the Temenggong was agreeable but had no power to authorize Raffles to do so. It was with the Temenggong's help that Hussein was brought to Singapore to be installed as sultan and to sign the agreement. Under the agreement, the sultan and the Temenggong would receive an annual allowance in return for allowing the British to establish a "factory" on Singapore island. More important, the agreement stated that no other powers were allowed to establish any settlements on any part of the island, thus fending off potential attacks from the Dutch.

Sir Thomas Stamford Raffles of the British East India Company, whose statue over-looks the Singapore River and the central business district, is most often known as the founder of modern Singapore. Courtesy of the author.

Raffles' unauthorized action infuriated the EIC officials and the Dutch. But the island was rapidly becoming too important for the British to lose. The import and export trade in Singapore was growing, and so was the population. The population had increased from 1,000 to 5,000 by 1821, with many migrants from the region attracted to Singapore by trading op-portunities. As a trading settlement, Singapore was, by many accounts, more successful than Penang because of its more strategic location on the India-China trade route and, more important, its status as a free port. Raffles in-sisted that Singapore remain a free port, with no taxes imposed on trade and industry carried out on the island. He believed that taxes were a hindrance to the island's development. The negative impact of taxes imposed on trade was illustrated by the case of Penang. Although Penang was initially a free port, the EIC introduced a 5 percent tax on trade in 1801 to offset administrative costs. The imposition of the taxes only further reduced Penang's attractive-ness as a trading center, which was already undercut by its extreme northerly position.

The tension between the British and the Dutch over the issue of Singapore was resolved by the 1824 Anglo Dutch Treaty (also known as the Treaty of London), which laid the basis for the division between modern Malaysia and Indonesia. The treaty split the region primarily into two spheres of influence—the Malay Peninsula went to the British and the Indonesian archipelago to the Dutch. Under this treaty, Singapore was recognized as British possession. In addition, Malacca was handed to the British, while Bencoolen, the British trading post in Sumatra, was given to the Dutch so that the territories would be on the right side of the division. In that same year, the British signed a treaty with Sultan Hussein that permanently ceded Singapore to the British.

For the first half of the 19th century, British interests in the Malay Peninsula were entrenched directly through the Straits Settlements, comprising Penang, Malacca, and Singapore. The Straits Settlements were formed in 1826 as a Crown Colony, administered separately from the other Malay states, with a focus on trade as the cornerstone of British policy in the Peninsula. The British also deliberately adopted a noninterventionist attitude toward local political affairs. As part of its mission to ensure peaceful relations with the local states, the British concluded the Burney Treaty of 1826 with Siam, which exerted control over the states of Kedah, Kelantan, and Terengganu. Like the 1824 Anglo-Dutch Treaty, the Burney Treaty spelled out the spheres of influence in the Malay Peninsula between the British and the Siamese. Under the treaty, the British accepted the Siamese suzerainty over Kedah, Kelantan, and Terengganu while the Siamese undertook not to extend their power beyond Perak. This understanding was critical in preventing conflicts and hostility between Siam and Britain over the Malay Peninsula in the ensuing century.

With the exception of the 1831–1832 Naning War that saw the Minangkabau state of Naning absorbed by Malacca, the British were generally reluctant to be politically involved in the Malay States as it was too financially costly. But increasing instances of civil wars and of territorial and succession disputes that had negative economic repercussions led British administrators and merchants to call on the British government to intervene to resolve the political instability. These disorders were largely a result of the changing economic situation. The large-scale opening of tin mines in Perak and Selangor in the 1850s and 1860s prompted attempts by rival groups of Chinese miners, backed by secret societies and local Malay chiefs, to gain control of the tin-producing districts. The frequency and scale of the fights escalated and began to spill over into the Straits Settlements. In one case, the fighting in Perak spilled over to Penang, sparking serious riots in 1867. The situation was further complicated by succession disputes in the various Malay states. The Straits Settlement merchants, fearing for their investments and commercial interests, petitioned the British government to intervene. In 1873, the newly arrived governor of the Straits Settlements, Sir Andrew Clarke, facilitated negotiations that resulted in the Pangkor Treaty of 1874.

The Treaty signaled a political shift in British-Malay relations and marked the start of a policy of more active British involvement in the Peninsula. It introduced the Residential System as a form of indirect British rule in which British Residents were appointed as advisers to the sultans of the Malay States. The Residents were to advise the rulers on all matters except religion. The main objectives of the system were to establish law and order, centralize the collection of revenue, and develop the resources of the state. The British saw it as a way

to preserve the accepted customs and traditions of the country, to enlist the sympathies, and interest of the people to our assistance, and to teach them the advantages of good government and enlightened policy.[10]

In reality, however, it was a case of the Residents ruling while the Malay sultans advised. The success of the Residential System was highly dependent on the personalities of the Residents, and their relationships with the sultans and the Malay chiefs. The system was more successful in some states than others. In Sungei Ujung (which later became part of the state of Negri Sembilan) and Selangor, for example, the Residents were personal friends of the rulers, which accounted for the relative success of the system in these states. It was a different story in Perak. Its Resident, J.W.W. Birch, was a forceful man who was not on friendly terms with the local chiefs. Historical records imply that Birch overstepped his advisory role and governed Perak like a British colony. It has been argued that his high-handed manners eventually led to his murder, in 1875, which ignited the Perak War that saw British troops sent in to quell the revolt. The development further entrenched British political involvement in the Peninsula.

British rule in the Peninsula continued to expand in the late 19th century. In 1896, the states of Perak, Pahang, Selangor, and Negri Sembilan were brought into a centralized administrative unit known as the Federated Malay States (FMS). The policy was a result of fears that these states were developing their own laws and policies under their respective Residents. Each Resident now reported to the Resident-General. Theoretically, each state was self-governing, and the sultans would retain their offices. The FMS was inaugurated on July 1, 1896. Shortly after, the four Siamese-controlled northern states of Terengganu, Kelantan, Perlis (carved out from Kedah), and Kedah also came under British control under the 1909 Anglo-Siamese Treaty. Under the treaty, Siam relinquished its control over these states while retaining control over Pattani, Narathiwat, Songkhla, Satun, and Yala (which are now part of modern Thailand). This treaty has been considered significant in establishing Siam as a buffer against the French in Indochina, keeping possible French encroachment on British possessions in Malaya in check. It also fixed the border between contemporary Malaysia and Thailand.

Terengganu, Kelantan, Perlis, and Kedah did not join the FMS but remained largely autonomous. Instead of Residents, these states accepted British-appointed Advisers. Together with Johor, which remained closely associated with the British and was autonomous, these four states were known as the Unfederated Malay States (UFMS). Although British land and tax reforms were introduced, the Malay ruling elites in these states enjoyed greater autonomy than their FMS counterparts. Among the Malay states, Johor was the most modern and unique. It was the last Malay state to receive a British Adviser—in 1914—and was the only Malay state that had its own military force and was able to fly the state flag together with the British Union Jack.

Sabah and Sarawak

Sarawak and Sabah developed very differently from the Peninsula. The two territories had been part of the Brunei Sultanate, whose power was declining by the 19th century. Both territories were initially ceded to individuals and run as private colonies before they were made British protectorates in 1888, together with Brunei. It was only after World War II that the two territories were transferred to the British Colonial Office as Crown Colonies.

Sarawak was ceded to the Briton James Brooke, a supporter of Raffles' idea of extending British influence in the region. Brooke first arrived in Borneo in 1839, when the sultan of Brunei was fighting revolts by the indigenous Dayaks and Malays. Brooke returned the following year and was given the governorship of Sarawak in return for helping the sultan put down the revolt. Brunei ceded the Sarawak to Brooke in 1846, giving him full control over the territory. Brooke subsequently established the Brooke dynasty, which ruled Sarawak for the next hundred years. He was known as the White Raja (White King). Under his successor and nephew, Charles, the boundaries of Sarawak were extended and British administration was formalized.

The area of present-day Sabah was first acquired by the U.S. consul in Brunei, Charles Lee Moses, in 1865. He later sold his rights to the Austrian consul, General Baron von Overbeck, in Hong Kong, who in turn formed a partnership with the British company Dent Brothers. Baron von Overbeck received full suzerainty over Sabah from the sultan of Brunei in 1877. In 1881, Dent bought out the Austrian consul general and formed the British North Borneo Chartered Company for the development North Borneo. Amid frequent tensions with the Brooke dynasty over territories, the company implemented an administrative structure similar to that which the British empire established in North Borneo.

Japanese Occupation

The Japanese Occupation between 1942 and 1945 was an important milestone. It happened at a time when British supremacy was increasingly being questioned, and it eventually undermined British standing in Malaya. On the day the Japanese bombed Pearl Harbor, they also landed in Kota Bahru, on the northeastern coast of the Malay Peninsula. Under the leadership of Lieutenant-General Tomoyuki Yamashita, known as the Tiger of Malaya, the Japanese troops rapidly progressed south toward Singapore. The British were not prepared. They had always expected any attack on Singapore—which was the great naval base for the British—to come from the sea. Instead, the Japanese made their way down the Peninsula on bicycles. By February 15, 1942, Singapore had surrendered, and the Japanese had captured Malaya in fewer than 100 days. Military historians consider the fall of British Malaya a military disaster.

Singapore, which the British regarded as "the impregnable fortress," fell to the Japanese on February 15, 1942. Singapore was renamed Syonan To, meaning Light of the South, and was made the center of the Japanese regional military administration in Malaya. Malaya was New Malai. In addition to worsening food shortages and living conditions, the war exacerbated the already festering ethnic tensions. During the occupation, the Japanese often used paramilitary units composed mainly of Malays to fight the Chinese-dominated resistance movement and encouraged the formation of Malay nationalist groups in return for Malay cooperation. The Japanese also nurtured Indian nationalist groups to resist British colonial rule in India. In contrast, the Chinese population of Malaya and Singapore bore the brunt of the brutality of the Japanese troops. The overseas Chinese support for the anti-Japanese resistance movement in China had been strong, and there were many active anti-Japanese elements in the Peninsula. In the first week of the Occupation, the Japanese conducted the Sook Ching (purification through purge) operation in Singapore in which all Chinese males between 18 and 50 years old were systematically rounded up. "Anti-Japanese elements" were identified and executed. Similar "mopping-up" exercises were conducted in the rural districts. There are disputes over the actual number of victims, but it is estimated that some 5,000 to 25,000 were killed in these operations.

The Postwar Years

Despite the initial euphoria at their return to Malaya, in September 1945, the British knew they could no longer stay on indefinitely as the ruling power, not just because of the increasing sense of nationalism but also because of their dwindling global influence. Postwar Britain could not keep up with the demands of an empire. The 19th century was the peak of the British empire, and it had exhausted the British politically and financially. As early as 1942, the British had already initiated plans for Malaya's eventual independence. In 1944, the British proposed the establishment of a Malayan Union that would consist of the Federated and Unfederated Malay states, Penang, and Malacca. Singapore, Sarawak, and North Borneo were not included in the new Union and were to remain as separate entities under British rule. The Malayan Union did not receive popular support from the Malay rulers; they were not consulted on it, and the proposal forced them to transfer their rights of legal sovereignty to the British. The Malayan Union turned what were formerly British protectorates into a collective British colony. Despite their misgivings, the rulers were forced into agreeing to abdicate their powers, and the Malayan Union was inaugurated on April 1, 1946. The Malay population was furious. Under the leadership of the Johor Mentri Besar (chief minister), Dato Onn bin Jaafar, the United Malays National Organization (UMNO) was formed to oppose the Malayan Union. Many British officers who served in Malaya were also against the Malayan Union.

Under pressure, the British drafted a new proposal. On February 1, 1948, the Federation of Malaya—comprising the nine Malay states, Penang, and Malacca—replaced the Malayan Union. Despite Singapore's demands to be included in the Federation, it was once again excluded. One of the reasons for Singapore's exclusion was the fear that the island's Chinese majority population would outnumber the Malays on the Peninsula. This ethnic tension had been exacerbated by wartime experiences. One of the main underground anti-Japanese movements was the Chinese and Communist-dominated Malayan People's Anti-Japanese Army (MPAJA), which conducted numerous hit-and-run attacks on the Japanese in both the city and in rural areas. In the immediate postwar years, the British relied on the MPAJA to maintain law and order as it was the only armed and well-organized group around. The MPAJA took this opportunity to exact revenge on its enemies and collaborators, many of whom were Malays. The communal killings only intensified the longstanding ethnic fears; the Malays considered the Chinese an economic threat, while the Chinese resented being treated as outsiders even though they had contributed to the economy of Malaya. Ironically, it was the fear of the Chinese majority of Singapore that would lead to Singapore's inclusion in the Federation of Malaysia in 1963.

The Emergency

The postwar years were turbulent, given the political changes and civil unrest. Between 1948 and 1960, Malaya and Singapore were in the throes of a Communist insurgency. The Communists adopted a policy of armed revolt; they attempted to disrupt the economy in a bid to discredit the British by attacking rubber plantations and tin mines in Malaya and fomenting strikes in Singapore. Their ultimate aim was to declare a Communist republic in Malaya. When attempts to use the labor movement in Singapore to unseat the British failed, the Communists retreated to the jungles of Malaya. It was from the jungles that the Communist Party of Malaya (MCP), under the leadership of Chin Peng, conducted a 12-year guerrilla war against the British. The jungle warfare prompted the British to declare a state of emergency in Malaya on June 18, 1948. The Emergency was to last for the next 12 years, or until 1960.

In the early years of the Emergency, the Communists relied on the Min Yuen, the people's organizations, for supplies, intelligence, and even arms. These organizations were based largely in the rural mining and agricultural estates. The British retaliated by adopting a combination of psychological warfare, supply cuts, and continued security measures to wear the Communists down. In a bid to cut off the Communists from their supply sources, the British built numerous protected settlements in the rural areas of Malaya. The British also introduced conscription for the military and police force to boost their strength. In 1955, the British and Malayan authorities held talks with the MCP. At the negotiations, known as the Baling Peace Talks, the British offered the Communists amnesty in return for surrender. But Chin Peng rejected the offer of amnesty. The talks broke down, and the Emergency continued. By the late 1950s, however, the Communists had already lost much ground. Local elections introduced in the late 1940s and early 1950s undermined the MCP's claims of fighting for independence, thus undercutting its credibility. Although the British declared the Emergency over on July 31, 1960, it was not until December 1989 that Chin Peng signed a peace treaty with Malaysia to officially end the armed conflict. Chin Peng and many former members of the MCP have since settled in southern Thailand. The Malaysian High Court has rejected Chin Peng's application to return to reside in Malaysia on the technical point that Chin had failed to show identification documents to prove his citizenship, which Chin said had been confiscated by the police in a 1948 raid.

Independence

The Emergency sped up negotiations for an independent Malaya. Discussions were under way to work on a constitutional settlement for a united

Malayan nation. The 1955 federal elections were a trial run for eventual self-government and independence. In the elections, the Alliance Party, comprising UMNO, the Malayan Chinese Association (MCA), and the Malayan Indian Congress (MIC), won decisively. The Alliance went on to form the first Malayan government under Tunku Abdul Rahman when Malaya was granted independence on August 31, 1957. In the following years, the Alliance expanded to include other non-Malay opposition parties. In 1973, the Alliance was succeeded by the Barisan Nasional (the National Front), which remains the ruling coalition in Malaysia today.

Separately, Singapore gained internal self-government in 1959 under the leadership of Lee Kuan Yew's People Action Party. One of main objectives of the new government was to gain independence from the British through merger with the Federation of Malaya. The leaders believed that Singapore was too small and resource-starved to be able to survive as an independent nation. Although there were discussions among the Malayan, British, and Singapore governments on the proposal for a merger, the first public mention of the possibility came from the Malayan prime minister, Tunku Abdul Rahman, at a meeting with foreign journalists in Singapore in May 1961.

Many Malayan leaders had misgivings about the inclusion of Singapore in any arrangements; they feared that the inclusion of the Chinese-dominated Singapore would threaten the numerical superiority of the Malays on the Peninsula. At the same time, however, they also feared a possibly Communist Singapore right at their doorstep. Although the Communists in Malaya had been defeated, the Communist movement remained strong in Singapore, dominating the trade unions, the Chinese schools, and even the political parties. On the other hand, some leaders believed that including Singapore in a federation of sorts would be the best way to contain the Communist elements. To overcome the fears of absorbing so many Chinese, it was proposed that the territories of British North Borneo and Sarawak be included in the new entity. There was strong political opposition to the merger within Singapore. The Communists feared that the merger would stifle their takeover of Singapore. The disagreement in the Singapore government between the pro-Communist and pro-merger factions led to a split in the ruling PAP and the formation of the opposition party Barisan Socialis. The Singapore public voted overwhelmingly for the merger in a contentious referendum in 1962. On August 31, 1963, the Federation of Malaysia—the political amalgamation of Malaya, Sabah, Sarawak, and Singapore—came into being. Brunei, also invited to join the Federation, had declined the invitation.

The Federation of Malaysia, however, came under pressure almost immediately. The Philippines and Indonesia were opposed to its formation. The Philippines contested Malaysia's territorial claims to Sabah, while Indonesia's

President Sukarno saw Malaysia as a threat to his dream of uniting the Malay world and forming a greater Indonesia. Indonesia's opposition took a violent turn with an armed campaign, Konfrontasi (Confrontation). During the two years of Konfrontasi, between 1963 and 1965, Indonesia launched incursions on the coast of Malaysia and on the borders of Sabah. Indonesian agents also exploded bombs in Singapore. The armed conflict ended only when the Indonesian president, Sukarno, was toppled from office, in 1965.

Domestically, Singapore's marriage with Malaya was also far from a happy affair. In the leadup to the formation of Malaysia, there were already acrimonious negotiations over the issues of finances, taxation, and trade between the leaders. Furthermore, both Singapore and the central government in Kuala Lumpur resented perceived intrusions in each other's politics. Singapore accused the Malay extremists of stirring up racial conflicts on the island, while the federal government feared that the PAP's participation in the 1964 federal elections would undercut Malay rule; it raised the specter, long feared by the Malays, of dominance by Singapore's Chinese. Against the backdrop of communal violence in 1963 and 1964, the PAP and the opposition parties in Sabah and Sarawak formed the Malaysian Solidarity Convention (MSC).

The MSC was formed to oppose affirmative action for the Malays, provided for under the Malaysian constitution. MSC leaders argued that such affirmative action was the basis of racial discrimination and that Malaysia should not be divided along ethnic lines—that Malaysia should be for Malaysians, not just the Malays. Yet, instead of reducing tensions, the move only served to widen the political rift between Singapore and the central government. Some UMNO leaders felt that the concept of a Malaysian Malaysia would undermine the special positions of the Malay, a fundamental premise of Malaysia. Attempts to resolve the differences failed. Eventually, the Malaysian prime minister, Tunku Abdul Rahman, suggested that it was in the interest of both Singapore and Malaysia to go their separate ways. On August 9, 1965, Lee Kuan Yew, the prime minister of Singapore, announced on national television the separation of Singapore from Malaysia. Singapore was an independent nation.

Two Independent Nations

Singapore and Malaysia are unique among the colonies in that their independence was the result of relatively amicable negotiations with the British and not of violent conflict, as was the case in many former colonies. Singapore was also unique in not wanting to have total independence because of the belief that it was "not viable by itself."[11] The initial postseparation years were difficult for both countries. As the Singapore leadership was still reeling from what it saw as a political failure, it also had to deal with an opposition that now attacked Singapore's independence as a sham development and claimed that it was a neocolonial state. The opposition, Barisan Socialis, sought to undermine the government through student movements as the Communists had in the 1950s. But the government moved to arrest the instigators of the protests and deported the noncitizens.

In addition to political troubles, the government also faced the critical issue of building up its economy, since the prospect of a common market with Malaysia was shattered by the separation. Singapore embarked on a program of rapid industrialization and undertook an aggressive plan to re-establish its traditional role as the region's financial, banking, and trading hub. The government intensified its efforts to woo local and foreign investments. In just two decades, the former British colony underwent dramatic changes in landscape, economy, standard of living, and lifestyle, transforming itself, as has been said, "from third world to first" and "from mangrove to metropolis."[12]

In the immediate postseparation years, Malaysia continued to be plagued by the communal issues. One main source of tension remained the special constitutional rights of the Malays. The rights were granted to the Malays by the 1948 constitution to safeguard their political position and to allow them to catch up with the Chinese and Indians, who were regarded as more economically successful. The other source of tension that had been simmering was the issue of education. The 1957 constitution recognized both Malay and English as the national languages, an arrangement that was to be reviewed after 10 years. The National Language Act of 1967, however, stipulated that Malay was the only official language, with English to be used only when necessary in the public interest.

The issue of education and national language became an election issue in 1969 when the Alliance government announced its intention to implement Malay as the sole medium of instruction at all schools levels, ultimately including university education. These tensions came to a head on May 13, 1963, when the UMNO-MCA-MIC Alliance lost its parliamentary majority to the opposition parties, Gerakan and the Democratic Action Party (DAP). The latter two had campaigned for the election on a platform of equal treatment of the races and had attracted substantial support from the Chinese and Indian communities. Gerakan and the DAP's victory rallies in Kuala Lumpur sparked counterdemonstrations by the Malays, which in turn led to several days of rioting. A state of emergency was declared and the constitution suspended. Almost 200 people were killed, and more than 400 were injured. Although the riots were under control within a couple of weeks, the state of emergency was not lifted until 1971.

The 1969 riots led to the introduction of a national ideology, the Rukunegara, in an attempt to promote national unity. Rukunegara promoted unity built on several fundamental concepts of Malaysian nationhood: respect for Islam and indigenous customs, loyalty to the king and the country, the supremacy of the constitution, the rule of law, and good social behavior. In the aftermath of the riots, the government also launched the New Economic Policy (NEP) to eliminate poverty and to erase ethnic identification with economic functions. Essentially, the NEP was a policy of affirmative action that favors the Malays through the policies of urbanizing the Malays and increasing their participation in commerce and industry. It remains in place till this day.

NOTES

1. Isabella L. Bird, *The Golden Chersonese and the Way Thither,* with an introduction by Wang Gungwu (Kuala Lumpur: Oxford University Press, 1967), p. 6.

2. Singapore Infomap, *Population Profile, 2007 Figures,* http://www.sg/explore/people_population.htm, accessed August 8, 2008.

3. Tourism Malaysia, *Fast Facts About Malaysia,* http://www.tourism.gov.my/en/about/facts.asp, accessed November 29, 2008.

4. United Nations Development Programme, *Malaysia Facts and Figures,* http://www.undp.org.my/resources/malaysia-facts-and-figures/malaysia-people, accessed November 29, 2008.

5. Swee Hock Saw, *The Population of Malaysia* (Singapore: Institute of Southeast Asian Studies, 2007), p. 5.

6. Mahathir Mohammad, *The Way Forward,* working paper presented at the Malaysian Business Council, http://www.pmo.gov.my/?menu=page&page=1904, accessed November 29, 2008.

7. C. C. Brown (trans.), *Sejarah Melayu, or Malay Annals* (Kuala Lumpur: Oxford University Press, 1970), p. 21.

8. Bird, *The Golden Chersonese,* p. 149.

9. Richard Winstedt, *A History of Malaya,* rev. ed. (Singapore: Marican & Sons, 1962), p. 162.

10. Barbara Watson Andaya and Leonard Andaya, *A History of Malaysia,* 2nd ed. (Honolulu: University of Hawaii Press, 2001), p. 174.

11. Mary Turnbull, *A History of Singapore 1819–1988,* 2nd ed. (Singapore: Oxford University Press, 1997), p. 288.

12. *The History of Singapore,* produced by Lion Television for Discovery Networks Asia (Singapore: Discovery Communications, 2006).

SUGGESTED READINGS

Andaya, Barbara Watson, and Leonard Andaya. *A History of Malaysia* (2nd edition). Honolulu: University of Hawaii Press, 2001.

Baker, Jim. *Crossroads: A Popular History Malaysia and Singapore* (2nd ed.). Singapore: Marshall Cavendish International, 2008.

Benjamin, Geoffrey, and Cynthia Chou (eds.). *Tribal Communities in the Malay World: Historical, Cultural and Sociological Perspectives.* Singapore: Institute of Southeast Asian Studies, 2002.

Farish A. Noor. *From Majapahit to Putrajaya: Searching for Another Malaysia.* Kuala Lumpur: Silverfish, 2005.

Funston, John (ed.). *Government and Politics in Southeast Asia.* Singapore: Institute of Southeast Asia Studies, 2001.

Hall, D. G. E. *A History of Southeast Asia.* London: Macmillan, 1968.

Raine, Nick, and Andy Raine. *Sabah. Sarawak: Land, People and Cultures.* Kuala Lumpur: S Abdul Majeed, 1995.

Sandhu, Kernial Singh, and Paul Wheatley (eds.). *Management of Success: The Moulding of Modern Singapore.* Singapore: Institute of Southeast Asian Studies, 1989.

Shennan, Margaret. *Out in the Midday Sun: The British in Malaya 1880–1960.* London: John Murray, 2000.

Turnbull, Mary. *A History of Singapore 1819–1988* (2nd ed.). Singapore: Oxford University Press, 1997.

2

Religion and Thought

IN SINGAPORE AND Malaysia, it is common to find mosques, temples, and churches side by side in the same areas. The multicultural and multiethnic nature of Singapore and Malaysia's societies is matched by an array of religions. Except for a handful of ethnic-related bursts of violence in the 1950s and 1960s, the various communities have coexisted peacefully, and people of different faiths interact with one another with ease. Religion is generally a private matter, and the various communities are identified more by their ethnicity than by their religion. Religion in Singapore and Malaysia is not strictly determined by or co-related to ethnicity. For example, Christianity extends across ethnic groups. The only exception is with the Malays, who are almost always Muslim. Islam (the religion) is not only the religion of the Malays; there are also Indian and Chinese Muslims.

The major religions practiced in Singapore and Malaysia are Islam, Christianity, Hinduism, and Chinese religions. There are also numerous other strands of minor religions and religious movements. Almost all the religions practiced in Singapore and Malaysia today are not indigenous to the region but were imported by the Indian and Arab traders, European colonialists, and Indian and Chinese migrants. Although similar to the religious practices in their respective home countries, the rites and rituals associated with these religions, as well as their meanings, have often been substantially localized over time. An interesting feature in the Singapore/Malaysia religious landscape is thus the syncretic nature of the religious practices; each religion has blended various influences from other religions to become a complex web of modified practices.

INDIGENOUS BELIEFS

Animism is the oldest strand of Malaysia's religious traditions and perhaps the only indigenous one. It was originally practiced in various permutations by the native tribes in Malaysia, including, to some extent, the Malays. More folk religion than institutionalized rituals, animism in the Peninsula is focused on the magical and is mainly concerned with the pragmatism of everyday life, "the specifics of man's worldly welfare."[1] These include praying for rain for crops, good harvests, treatments for illnesses, and even for success in one's personal life in love and revenge. Unlike most other religions that deal with morality, ethics, and salvation, animism is not concerned with the afterlife or with the future. Instead, it is considered a very present help in trouble. It is this feature of animism that explains the necessity of the existence of the *bomoh* (healer or doctor) or the *pawang* (individual who performs magical practices). These individuals, akin to priests, are the bridges between the humans and the spirits. Despite being known by different names, these individuals nevertheless hold important positions, especially in the rural areas. The *pawang*s are generally regarded as conduits to the spirits and are called upon to officiate at religious ceremonies and harvest rituals.

One of the key features of animism is belief in the existence of spirits. Animists believe that the natural environment is populated with an array of spirits, both malicious and kind, who can bring either ill luck or good fortune. These spirits are believed to reside in almost everything, including rivers, trees, flowers, stones, and air. As the British colonial official Sir Richard Winstedt wrote in his classic text on Malay animism, evil spirits

lurk everywhere: on top of palmyra trees, in caves and rocks, in ravines and chasms. They fly about in the air, like birds of prey, ready to pounce down upon any unprotected victim.[2]

This feature of animism is related to the belief in *semangat,* which means the soul or vital substance that is endowed in all living and nonliving things. As it is considered the source of all life, the *semangat* is both feared and revered. It is thus common for many tribes to hold seasonal feasts and ceremonies to invoke their aid or to give thanks for their help. One of the most highly revered *semangat* is that of the *padi* (rice), which is the basic food of the Malay. There is an elaborate set of rituals related to the rice fields. Agriculturalist tribes typically have the *pawang* (magician) perform various rites before planting and during the harvesting of the rice crop, including one to expel evil spirits before the clearing of the land. At harvest time, the magician has to "take the souls of the rice" and cast out evil spirits before the crops are gathered. In certain parts of the Peninsula, harvest dances are also part of the harvesting processes, with some lasting for days.

Like many aspects of the Peninsula's culture and customs, animism in the region is a fusion of indigenous beliefs and Hindu and Islamic elements. One of the clearest examples of this is *keramat* worship, which is the worship of persons of high religious standing or their graves. Devotees usually pray for their wishes, mainly practical, related to their daily lives, such as the healing of illnesses and blessings for their families. One popular *keramat* in Singapore is the Keramat Iskandar Shah at Fort Canning, which is believed to be the burial place of the founding ruler of the Malacca Sultanate, Parameswara, as he was known before his conversion to Islam. *Keramat* worship is not only limited to the Malays, although orthodox Muslims see it as an undesirable practice in Islam. Chinese and Indians are also known to practice *keramat* worship, especially in Singapore.

ISLAM

Islam is the official religion of Malaysia and one of the main religions in Singapore. About 15 percent of Singapore's and about 60 percent of Malaysia's populations are Muslim. Although Islam is a major religion in the Singapore/ Malaysia cultural landscape, it is not an indigenous religion. Arab and Indian merchants who were actively trading in the area brought Islam to the Malay Peninsula from as early as the 11th century. But it was only in the 14th century that Islam became the region's principal religion, its rise coinciding with the decline of the Buddhist Srivijaya and Hindu Majapahit empires. Historians have generally attributed the spread and establishment of Islam in the Malay Peninsula to Parameswara, the founder of the Malacca Sultanate, who converted to Islam in 1414 in order to marry a Muslim princess. Other scholars, however, have pointed out that Parameswara's conversion was a personal choice and had little bearing on the state religion, which remained Hinduism. It was not until the reign of Sultan Mansur Shah (1459–1477) that Islam replaced Hinduism as the official religion of the Malacca Sultanate. Islam gradually spread to its surrounding vassal states of Pahang, Kedah, Terengganu, Kelantan, and Patani.

The discovery of a stone inscribed with Jawi writings in the northeast Malaysian state of Terengganu, however, seems to indicate that Islam was already established in the Peninsula almost a century before Parameswara's conversion. The stone, known as the Terengganu Inscription Stone, was discovered in the late 19th century. Dated 1303, the stone contains Jawi inscriptions of local laws influenced by the Islamic Syariah law. It is perhaps the earliest physical evidence of Islam as the official religion of Terengganu by the early 14th century. Today, the stone is on display at the National History Museum in Malaysia's capital.

The majority of Muslims in Singapore and Malaysia are Sunni Muslims of the Shafi school. Like most of the Sunni Muslims around the world, they subscribe to five pillars of faith that guide their personal and social conduct. The first pillar of Islam is *syahadat,* the profession of faith. This declaration states that that the only purpose of life is to serve and obey God, and this is achieved through obedience to the teachings and practices (as stated in *Quran* and *Sunnah*) of the Prophet Muhammad. The *syahadat*—"I bear witness that there is no God worthy of worship but Allah and Muhammad is the Messenger of God"—is recited in the daily prayers and is a requirement for a convert in affirming his earnestness in the conversion. The second pillar is prayer, which is obligatory for all Muslims. Orthodox Muslims pray five times a day: before sunrise, around noon, around four in the evening, at sunset, and just before bedtime. Muslims can pray anywhere, in private or in a congregation. The only rule is that it must be done facing the direction of Mecca, Islam's holy city. Every Friday across Singapore and Malaysia, calls to prayers are broadcast from mosques, calling all adult male Muslims to attend noon prayers. Fasting or *puasa* is the third pillar of Islam. Muslims worldwide fast throughout the month of Ramadan, the ninth month in the Islamic calendar. This is a month of spiritual cleansing, and fasting is an extension of the process of cleansing oneself. During the fast, which begins at sunrise, no food or drink is allowed. The fast is broken only at sunset. The end of Ramadan is marked by Hari Raya Puasa (Aidil Fitri) celebrations.

The fourth pillar of Islam is *zakat,* a form of tithing. Muslims are encouraged to donate 2.5 percent of their wealth annually as *zakat* to help the poor and needy. In addition, *zakat* beneficiaries include those appointed to undertake tasks associated with *zakat* collection, new converts, captives (to pay for their ransoms) debtors (to relieve their debts), the *fi-sabilillah* (those who work in the cause of Allah), and those who are stranded and need assistance to reach their destination. The final pillar of Islam is the *haj,* or pilgrimage to Mecca. Muslims are encouraged to undertake the pilgrimage at least once in their lifetime. The *haj* is obligatory for the financially and physically able. For the Muslim, the *haj* is an opportunity to pursue a spiritual experience in being close to Allah and his Prophets, as well as to seek forgiveness for one's sins.

In recent years, Singapore and Malaysia have experienced a surge of Islamic fundamentalism. Shortly after the September 11, 2001, attacks in the United

States, Singapore arrested members of an Islamic fundamentalist group, Jemmah Islamiah, with links to Al Qaeda. Dozens of members were also arrested in Malaysia. Home to a substantial Muslim community, Singapore and Malaysia are eager to distance themselves from the extremist branches of Islam. Leaders of both countries have spoken out against religious extremists and have sought to assure the Muslim community that counterterrorism measures are not targeted at the community or Islam.

The rise in religious conservatism is also seen in the more ordinary day-to-day livelihood of the people. The most obvious change is in the appearance of the Muslims. Increasingly, more Muslim women in Singapore and Malaysia are wearing the *tudung,* a headscarf that conceals the hair but not the face, and clothes that show only their hands, according to the Islamic dress code. The numbers of Muslim men sporting a beard—a sign of their religion—are also on the rise. While it is not mandatory for Muslim men to grow beards, it is often encouraged, as Prophet Muhammad also kept a beard. Another visible sign of religiosity is the increase in the number of *halal* (food that is free of port and alcohol and that is prepared in a prescribed manner) eating outlets in Singapore and Malaysia.

With the rise of religious conservatism, more and more Muslim women in Singapore and Malaysia are wearing the *tudung,* a headscarf that conceals the hair. Courtesy of the author.

One longstanding debate in Malaysia is whether the country is an Islamic state. Although the Malaysian constitution declares that Malaysia is a secular state, in recent years, some Muslim groups have pressed the government to proclaim Malaysia an Islamic state. They argue that since Muslims are the majority and Article 3 of its constitution states that Islam is the state religion, Malaysia therefore should be an Islamic state. These groups ultimately want Malaysia to be governed by Islamic laws. Although there is not yet an official declaration of the government's stand on the issue, some politicians have commented that Malaysia is a moderate Islamic state, adding to the confusion and dissatisfaction of the non-Muslim population.

CHINESE RELIGIONS

It is difficult to distinguish among the various Chinese religions practiced in Singapore and Malaysia. Unlike Islam, for example, the Chinese religion does not have a formal organized structure. Thus, while many Chinese may identify themselves as Taoists or Buddhists, in actuality, the distinction is often hard to make. Very rarely are the adherents purely either Taoist or Buddhist in their practices. More often than not, their practices blend in with local beliefs and practices, such as *keramat* worship. There are also adherents of "pure" Buddhism and Taoism, but their numbers are small. In this section, the term "Chinese religion"—used by sociologists to describe the syncretic nature of religious practices and beliefs of the Chinese in Singapore and Malaysia—refers to the various belief systems of the Chinese. The section also outlines some of Chinese religion's significant features.

Chinese folk religion accompanied the waves of Chinese migrants who came to Singapore and Malaysia in the 19th century. Just like the social aspect of their lives, Chinese religious life was closely aligned with their dialect and regional affiliations. Each dialect group built its own temples and developed its own religious community. For example, in Singapore, there are various Chinese temples identified with the various dialect groups, including the Hengshan Ting (Hokkiens), Wak Hai Cheng Bio (Teochews), Haichun Fude Si (Cantonese), Yinghe Guan (Hakkas), and Tianhou Temple (Hainanese).

The majority of the Chinese migrants were of the peasant class, and they brought with them the folk beliefs of their homeland. Like the indigenous animistic beliefs, the Chinese folk beliefs are not monotheist in nature. Instead, the Chinese believe that different deities with different powers guard the various aspects of life. There is a huge pantheon of Chinese deities, but the most commonly worshipped ones are Guan Gong (God of War), Guan Yin (Goddess of Mercy), Dabogong (Earth God), and Mazu (Goddess of Sea). These deities may reside in dedicated temples or share residences with other deities. Most Chinese homes also house altars to these deities, the most common of which are the Goddess of Mercy, the Earth God, and the Kitchen God.

Most adherents of Chinese folk religion are not particular about visiting only a specific temple. Often, they visit various temples housing their patron deities when the need arises. Prayers are not obligatory. Adherents can visit the temples as often or as infrequently as they like, although most make it a point to visit on festive occasions such as the birthdays of the deities. In temples, incense and prayers are offered, a process that takes only minutes. Sometimes believers also have their fortunes told through the use of fortune sticks (*qiu qian*). Believers shake a canister that holds the fortune sticks in the presence of the deity until a single stick falls out. They then take the stick to the fortune teller, who reads them the corresponding fortune according to the questions asked.

Regardless of the various theological tenets, one of the most important elements of the Chinese religion is that of ancestor worship. This practice is often regarded as an extension of the critical value of filial piety in Chinese culture. It includes the rituals of offering incense and food at the ancestor's altar, normally found in most Chinese households or, in some cases, in temples. On important occasions, such as the ancestors' birth and death anniversaries, and during important festivals, living descendents prepare more elaborate offerings. In addition to feasts of meat, fish, fruits, and the deceased's favorite foods, paper money and/or paper models of material goods, such as houses, cars, servants, and even electronic goods like television and radio sets, are burnt and "sent" to the deceased forebears. In return, the ancestors, like the pantheon of Chinese deities, provide protection and guidance for their descendants.

Taoism

Taoism, generally, is a school of Chinese philosophy believed to be founded by Lao Zi, who lived in the 6th century B.C. There are some debates among scholars about whether Lao Zi was a historical figure or a legendary one. Regardless, his teachings took root and evolved into Taoism. Taoism is concerned with the relation between human beings and Nature. One of its key ideas is the notion of balance, reflected in the concept of *yin* and *yang*. Taoists believe that balance is regulated by Tao (often translated as "The Way"), a force that flows through all things. It is believed that the Tao is expressed in virtue through naturalness (*ziran*) and nonaction (*wuwei*). Scholars have struggled with and debated what the Tao is concretely and what the Taoist text, the *Daodejing* (*Classic of the Way and Virtue*), meant by naturalness and nonaction. Many of the Taoist concepts are vague and often open to interpretation. It is this vagueness that has led some people to associate Taoism with mysticism.

Taoism has a religious aspect (commonly referred to as *daojiao*). The often mystical sages of the Taoist philosophy have, over time, been elevated to the status of deities, with dedicated temples and associated rites and rituals. As in Catholicism and Christianity, there are ordained priests who perform highly ritualized ceremonies, such as funeral rites. As a religion, Taoism is often regarded as a folk religion, with its large pantheon of deities, who may be either literary or historical figures. Taoism has, over the centuries, absorbed external influences from Buddhism and Confucianism, for example, into its beliefs and practices. About 8.5 percent of Singapore's population consider themselves Taoist, while the number is considerably smaller in Malaysia, hovering around 2.6 percent, including those who practice "other traditional Chinese religions," according to the 2000 census.[3]

Buddhism

Buddhism was brought to the Malay Peninsula by the pilgrims who traveled to and from India, the holy land of Buddhism. Together with Hinduism, Buddhism was one of the most lasting effects of what has been termed "Indianization"—the process by which cultural and religious influences from India spread throughout Southeast Asia between the 1st and the 12th centuries. The two main schools of Buddhism are Mahayana and Hinayana (or Theravada) Buddhism, both of which spread throughout Southeast Asia. By about the fourth century, Buddhism was already established in parts of the Malay Peninsula. Inscriptions of Buddhist verses dated to the fourth and fifth centuries have been found in the Malaysian state of Kedah. The maritime empire of Srivijaya was recognized as the center of Buddhism in the region, and it is possible that the Buddhist influence spilled over to its territories in the Peninsula.

Buddhism, like Hinduism, was found only in the center of royal power, usually far removed from commerce. These two religions introduced the idea of divine kingship, which was adopted by the Malay rulers of Srivijaya and, later, the Malay states. That was where the influence of Buddhism ended; it "hardly extended beyond courts and ports, the peasant of the interior still remaining an animist and ancestor-worshipper with a mythology of his own."[4] Buddhism in Singapore and Malaysia today has been developed from the earlier forms into one with more popular appeal to the masses. Today about 43 percent of Singapore's population and about 20 percent of Malaysia's population consider themselves Buddhist.[5]

One major Buddhist movement in Singapore and Malaysia is the Soka Gakkai movement. Originating in Japan, the Soka Gakkai movement has

Buddhism was initially a court religion. Over the centuries, it has developed into one with a popular appeal to the masses. Courtesy of the author.

its philosophical base in the Nichiren Soshu branch of Japanese Buddhism. This branch of Buddhism draws its inspiration from the 13th-century Buddhist monk Nichiren Daishonin. The key philosophical tenets of the Soka Gakkai movement include strong commitment to harmonious societies, cultural understanding, and education. Although the Soka Gakkai movement is religious, both the Singapore Soka Association (SSA) and the Soka Gakkai Malaysia (SGM) are active, grassroots-based organizations. SSA, for example, contributes large contingents that perform in Singapore's annual National Day Parade and the Chingay Parade. Similarly, SGM conducts regular community activities such as family days, cultural exchanges, exhibitions, and seminars. Both SSA and SGM are associates of Soka Gakkai International.

Core Buddhist Concepts

Buddhism is more akin to a philosophy than a religion. It does not have a set of ritualistic practices (except the chanting of the Scriptures, usually practiced by monks and nuns) to which its believers must strictly adhere. Instead, the Buddhist faith is premised on several key concepts. The Four Noble Truths are one of the most critical. It states that:

Suffering exists;
Suffering arises from attachment to desires;
Suffering ceases when attachment to desire ceases; and
Freedom from suffering is possible by practicing the Eightfold Path.

The Four Noble Truths and the Eightfold Path constitute the gist of Buddhism. The Eightfold Path is a set of practical guidelines believed to enable one to end suffering through the development of one's ethics and mental strength. The ultimate goal of the Path is to liberate the individual from attachments and delusions, which will finally lead one to an understanding of the Truth. The eight aspects of the path are having the right view, the right intention, the right speech, the right action, the right livelihood, the right effort, the right mindfulness, and the right concentration. These aspects of ethical conduct and mental development can be achieved through meditation and are not interdependent. Buddhists believe that Path will help believers overcome the five hindrances of life: lust; aversion and ill will; slothfulness; restlessness and worry; and doubts.

Hinduism

Like Buddhism, Hinduism is one of the earliest religions to take root in the Malay Peninsula. The influence of India and the Srivijaya and Majapahit Empires were critical. The earliest form of Hinduism that was brought to the Malay Peninsula was Brahmanic Hinduism, a branch closely associated with the Hindu priestly caste (Brahmin). The early Malacca Sultanate is perhaps the best example of Hindu influence in the Malay Peninsula. Traces of Hindu influence can still be found in the Malay language and in Malay literature and art. The Hinduism practiced in Singapore and Malaysia today is, however, of a different branch and was brought here by the Indian settlers who came to the region in the late 19th and early 20th centuries.

Hinduism is a ritualistic religion. For Hindus, there are 16 Vedic *samskara*s (rites or rituals) in the life of an individual, relating to marriage, pregnancy, the birth of a child, confinement, retirement, and death. But with rapid modernization and the fast pace of life, many Hindus today perform these rites either selectively or not at all. Furthermore, most Hindus today perform these rites more as social obligations rather than as religious duties. Like the Chinese religion, Hinduism is polytheistic. A Hindu can worship several deities, as they are seen as representations of one true God, who in its various forms can grant worshippers grace to bring them closer to *moksha* (the end of the cycle of rebirth). The gods Brahma (the Creator), Vishnu (the Preserver), and Shiva (the Destroyer), together with their consorts Saraswathi (Goddess of Knowledge), Lakshmi (Goddess of Wealth), and Parvathi (Goddess of Power), are the most popular Hindu deities.

Forms of Worship

Hindu worship can take place both at the temple or at home. Several types of rituals take place at the temple—daily rituals, those performed on specific occasions, such as during festivals, and voluntary rituals. The basic rituals performed daily at many Hindu temples include waking the deity at dawn, preparing the deity for worship and offerings by visitors at midday, and putting the deity to bed in the evening. Some temples also have additional rituals of bathing and feeding the deity. A visitor to a temple can also request *puja* (daily prayers) in return for a donation. Hindu temples used to be an integral part of Hindu life in the early days, as they acted as community spaces and welfare centers. With improved welfare and social services, the influence of the temple has been reduced. Today Hindus are able to congregate elsewhere for the nonreligious events that used to be hosted at the temples. But the temple is still an important place of Hindu worship and remains at the heart of festivals and traditional ceremonies, although many of these are now celebrated on a smaller scale than previously.

Worship may also be performed at home. In many Hindu households, for example, it is common to find a dedicated space for the family deity. Prayers and offerings, including the lighting of a lamp, are made in front of the shrine. Dawn and dusk are the two most important times of the day for the performance of these rituals. Traditionally, the day starts with the women drawing art (*kolam*) on the floor or the doorstep with chalk or rice flour. This practice is becoming rare and is now usually performed on special festive days.

Fasting is also part of the Hindu religious practice. According to the Hindu belief, fasting has a way of neutralizing or minimizing chaos in the body. When an individual fasts, his mind is focused not on food but on spirituality. Hindus fast when they are fulfilling a vow or observing a holy day. Hindu fasting need not mean a total abstinence from food. A simple fast consists of simply avoiding certain foods for the duration of the fast (which can be a day or more). For example, nonvegetarians abstain from meat. A more moderate fast might involve avoiding rich food or having only liquids to keep the body as "clean" as possible.

The Batu Caves in Kuala Lumpur, Malaysia, are a holy site for Hindus in Malaysia. The Temple Cave at the top of the 272 steps houses a shrine dedicated to the Hindu deity Lord Subramaniam, also known as Lord Murugan. Courtesy of the author.

The Satya Sai Baba Movement

Disputed by Hindus as a branch of Hinduism and often branded a cult by others, the Satya Sai Baba movement is an intriguing religious movement. It is centered around the South Indian religious guru, Satya Sai Baba. Born Narayana Raju in 1926 in South India, Sai Baba claims to be an incarnation of the original 19th-century Indian guru and yogi Sai Baba of Shirdi. The 20th-century reincarnate was said to have displayed extraordinary powers as a child and is often described as a miracle worker. He also claimed to be an incarnation of two Hindu deities, Shiva and Shakti. The primary teachings of Sathya Sai Baba emphasize the unity and equality of all religions, service and charity (*seva*) to others, limiting one's desires, vegetarianism, abstinence from alcohol, cigarettes and drugs, and detachment from the material world. It also teaches that every creature and object is God in a different form. Although not fully supported by the Hindu community and having been embroiled in scandals relating to the misconduct of Sai Baba himself, the movement has a substantial following in Singapore and Malaysia. Among the devotees are a large number of Chinese.

CHRISTIANITY

The different strands of Christianity were introduced to the Malay Peninsula by the Europeans. Among them, Catholicism is the oldest, brought to the region by the Portuguese when they conquered the city of Malacca in the 16th century. Portuguese Malacca became a major center of missionary activities in Asia, although for many missionaries—including St. Francis Xavier, one of the founders of the Jesuits—Malacca was not a destination but a port of call en route to China and Japan. Nevertheless, Malacca became a Catholic city in its own right. By the time Malacca fell to the Dutch, in 1641, there were more than 20,000 Catholics in the city, served by 19 churches, a cathedral, and numerous chapels. Evidence of Malacca's Catholic identity can still be seen today in the ruins of a church built in 1590 by the Jesuits on St. Paul's Hill. After being suppressed by the Dutch, who introduced Protestant Christianity to the region, Catholicism returned to prominence in the 19th century.

Over the course of the 19th and early 20th centuries, Protestant Christianity followed. Among the major schools of Protestant Christianity are the Presbyterian, Methodist, Baptist, and Anglican Churches. Churches and cathedrals were built in various urban centers throughout the Peninsula. The missionaries also set up schools. For the missionaries, the schools were instruments of evangelism, while the locals saw English education as a path to a better future. But even as Christianity was taking root in the Malay Peninsula and gaining many converts, particularly among the Chinese and the Indians, the missionaries were prohibited by the 1874 Pangkor Treaty from evangelizing to the Malays, who adhered to Islam.

Today, about 14.6 percent of Singapore's and 9.1 percent of Malaysia's populations are of the Christian faith.[6] The key rituals are similar to those practiced in Western countries. The Catholics, for example, are obliged to participate in congregational mass once a week and on specific holy days in the Catholic calendar, such as Ascension Day, All Saints Day, Good Friday, Easter Sunday, and Christmas Day. Most Christians attend church on Sunday for worship and sermons. In addition to English, the church services are often held in various languages and dialects, such as Hokkien, Cantonese, and even Tagalog and Burmese for the foreign congregations. It is also not unusual for the churches to host several services at various times for different groups. Like other religions, Christianity and Catholicism in Singapore and Malaysia contain certain degrees of religious syncretism. In the case of Chinese Catholics, holy water is sprinkled at homes to ward off evil spirits, and people wear images of Christ or the Virgin Mary as amulets to protect them from harm. Some Christians also participate in rites and rituals ascribed to the Chinese communities, such as ancestor worship. On the other hand, staunch Christians consider such localized practices unacceptable.

Christianity is experiencing a revival, especially among teenagers and young adults, in Singapore. One of the reasons for this is the growing number of new and independent churches, which are more evangelical in nature. Many of these churches also have a more progressive and "funky" image, which attracts the youth. These churches, mostly of the Pentecostal or Charismatic movement, have worship sessions, led by charismatic worship leaders with a troop of backup singers, that are akin to pop concerts, with drums, electric guitars, and keyboards. The pastor of one rapidly growing church is a popular Mandarin singer who has made a foray into the American music industry. In another case, the pastor of a successful church teamed up with his daughter to perform magic shows that have wowed international audiences. These new churches have also reached out to the society in various ways. Many of them have established welfare arms to help the terminally ill, the elderly, the needy, and low-income families. Another reason for the religious revival in Singapore and Malaysia is that religion is regarded as the moral guardian of the people. The Singapore government, especially, sees religion as a repository of morality and ethics and therefore encourages the various communities to utilize their creeds for their spiritual and moral benefits. Religion is also closely linked to a community's identity. It gives believers a sense of belonging to a community through their values, rites and rituals, and beliefs.

Asian Values

In the early 1990s, Singapore's and Malaysia's political leaders championed the concept of "Asian values." The concept was strongly supported by Singapore's Lee Kuan Yew and Malaysia's Mahathir Mohammad, both former prime ministers. The Asian values debate was a reaction to the rapid Westernization of Singapore and Malaysian societies. Western culture, including Hollywood movies, fast-food chains, pop culture, and Western attitudes, were increasingly becoming the mainstay of the cultural landscape in the 1980s. Even today, young people in Singapore and Malaysia are as familiar with the characters of popular American television productions such as *Friends* and *American Idol* as their American counterparts. The political leaders were worried about the impact of such pervasive Western influence. The Western tradition of favoring the individual over the collective was regarded as negating the strong collective interests favored by the governments. While not totally dismissing Western culture, the Singapore and the Malaysian governments wanted to address what they saw as "defects" in Western ideas.

"Asian values" were also used as a defense against the torrent of Western criticisms of authoritarianism in both countries. Although Singapore and Malaysia have features of democracy, such as regular elections, both governments have often been viewed as semi-authoritarian states that are not truly democratic. In response to criticisms that the governments were "iron hands in velvet gloves," Singapore and Malaysia used the concept of "Asian values" to challenge the cultural and ideological dominance of Western liberal democracy.[7] Against the backdrop of their economic successes, the political leaders used "Asian values" as a justification for alternative political-social systems in which high living standards and authoritarian politics coexisted. "Asian values" were also seen as an antidote to the ills of Western society, cited by local politicians as "guns, drugs, violent crime, vagrancy, unbecoming behaviour in public—in sum, the breakdown of civil society."[8]

There are no written tenets of these "Asian values," although there have been academic and political publications on the issue. Generally, Asian values are said to include the Confucian ethics of obedience to authority and strong central rule. Although Confucianism is often identified with the Chinese, the values it espouses—obedience, social hierarchy, and respect for authority, for example—are considered "Asian." Furthermore, Confucianism is seen more as a philosophy guiding human relations than as a religion, which makes it a more suitable and neutral ideological basis for guiding social behavior than religion. Collective interests, such as national economic development and social order, are given priority over individual rights.

The clearest explanation of Asian values can be found in the Shared Values White Paper authored by the Singapore government in 1991 to locate "the characteristic ethos and spirit of a people." It lists five core values: nation before community and society before self; the family as the basic unit of society; community support and respect for the individual; consensus not conflict; and racial and religious harmony. These "Asian values" were promoted as the basis of Singapore's national ideology. The concept of Asian values is a controversial one and has fallen out of favor since the 1997 Asian financial crisis. Still, it remains a critical concept in understanding the philosophical and political attitudes of the Singapore and Malaysian governments.

NOTES

1. Susan E. Ackerman and Raymond L. M. Lee, *Heaven in Transition: Non-Muslim Religious Innovation and Ethnic Identity in Malaysia* (Honolulu: University of Hawaii Press, 1988), p. 13.

2. Richard Winstedt, *The Malay Magician,* rev. ed. (London: Routledge, 1951), p. 4.

3. Department of Statistics, Singapore, *Census of Population 2000, Advance Data Release No. 9: A Decade of Progress* (Singapore: Department of Statistics, 2001); Department of Statistics Malaysia, *Population Distribution and Basic Demographic Characteristics* (Malaysia: Department of Statistics, 2001).

4. Richard Winstedt, *A History of Malaya* (revised and enlarged) (Singapore: Marican & Sons, 1962), p. 29.

5. Singapore Infomap Web site, http://www.sg/SG_Glance/people.htm, and CIA World Factbook, https://www.cia.gov/library/publications/the-world-factbook/geos/my.html, both sites accessed November 29, 2008.

6. Singapore Infomap Web site, http://www.sg/SG_Glance/people.htm, and CIA World Factbook, https://www.cia.gov/library/publications/the-world-factbook/geos/my.html, both sites accessed November 28, 2008.

7. Ien Ang and Jon Stratton, "The Singapore Way of Multiculturalism: Western Concepts/Asian Cultures," *Sojourn* 10, no. 1 (1995): 65–89.

8. Fareed Zakaria, "Culture Is Destiny—A Conversation with Lee Kuan Yew," *Foreign Affairs* 73, no. 2 (March/April 1994): 111.

SUGGESTED READINGS

Ackerman, Susan, and Raymond Lee. *Heaven in Transition: Non-Muslim Religious Innovation and Ethnic Identity in Malaysia.* Honolulu: University of Hawaii Press, 1988.

Clammer, John. *Singapore: Ideology, Society, Culture.* Singapore: Chopmen, 1985.

Fealy, Greg, and Virginia Hooker (eds.). *Voices of Islam in Southeast Asia: A Contemporary Sourcebook.* Singapore: Institute of Southeast Asia Studies. 2006.

McDougall, Colin. *Buddhism in Malaya.* Singapore: D. Moore, 1956.

Ong, Y. *Buddhism in Singapore: A Short Narrative History.* Singapore: Skylark, 2005.

Pas, Julian F., in cooperation with Man Kam Leung. *Historical Dictionary of Taoism.* London: Scarecrow Press, 1998.

3

Literature, Arts, and Crafts

SINGAPORE AND MALAYSIA have a rich history in literature, arts, and crafts. Before the arrival of Islam, myths and stories inspired by animism and Hinduism were popular. These stories were forms of entertainment and moral instruction and were spread through storytellers, dance performances, and theater. The arrival of Islam encouraged the adoption of Arabic script and the writing down of religious instructions so that they could be accurately disseminated. Soon, ancient myths and stories were also written down, but often with the intent that they be read aloud in a group as the overall level of literacy was still low. Literacy improved with the spread of education during the period of British colonization, and the introduction of printing increased access to reading materials. Both Singapore and Malaysia now have high literacy rates; newspapers, magazines, and books are written and published in the main languages. However, in modern Singapore and Malaysia, many local writers now prefer to write in English in order to be accessible across ethnic groups. In addition, many of the younger generation are educated in English and are more comfortable expressing themselves in this language.

Arts and crafts have long been part of the traditions of the indigenous and Malay communities, which have recognized expertise in fields such as woodcarving, weaving, and silversmithing. Many of these time-consuming handmade items are now replaced by mass-produced, factory-made counterparts that are cheaper and far less time-consuming to produce. Nevertheless, traditional arts and crafts remain an important part of the indigenous and Malay cultural identity, and they continue to be practiced by dedicated groups of artisans. In recent years, the Malaysian government has actively supported these traditional crafts and craftsmen through various schemes such as awarding master craftsmen national honors. Despite these incentives, there are few young people who are willing to learn these skills.

In both countries, there is a growing interest in Western-style visual arts such as painting, sculpture, and printmaking. Since the 20th century, many local artists have traveled and studied abroad, bringing back new ideas and perspectives about art. Contemporary Singapore and Malaysian artists are active in practicing new artistic forms such as installation, performance, and digital art to express their ideas and aesthetics on a range of personal, national, and transnational issues by experimenting with old and new forms, materials, and motifs.

TRADITIONAL LITERATURE

Traditional literature in Singapore and Malaysia not only refers to written forms but covers a wide range of oral literary creations including animal, humor and wit stories; myths; legends; sayings; *pantun* (a Malay poetic form); and the *adat* (customary laws). The earliest literary works have animistic and Hindu origins. While many were based on tales from Hindu classics such as the *Ramayana* and *Mahabharata,* they also included the *lipur lara* stories— tales of romance and adventure concerning princes and princesses that have happy endings. Animal stories were also common, the most popular revolving around the mousedeer, or *Sang Kancil*, who is able to outsmart animals much larger and stronger than she is, such as the crocodile (*buaya*). The authors of these stories are unknown, and these works are regarded as a collective creation of the community.

Poetry was part of the early literary tradition. Some of the earliest verses were spells and incantations composed and chanted by the Malay shamans to communicate with the spiritual world. A predominant poetic form is the *pantun,* a four-line verse or quatrain that consists of roughly alternately rhyming lines—an a-b-a-b rhyme scheme. The first two lines are called the *pembayang maksud* (foreshadower) and the third is the *maksud* (purpose). The poem wraps up with a profound, witty, or emotionally true conclusion. Natural imagery is used to suggest their meaning, and the form has been described as "remarkably crisp, often extremely colorful and passionate, sometimes bitterly cynical and it says a great deal in a very small space."[1] Another popular poetic form is the *syair*, which is more narrative than the *pantun*. It is a versatile form of poetry in which each line generally comprises four words. In its simplest form, verses consist of four lines that rhyme. The earliest *syairs* were represented by the works of Hamzah Fansuri, a Malay Sufi poet of the 17th century who is reputed to be creator of the genre.

Traditionally, poetry, stories, and folklores were transmitted orally. They were told, retold, and embellished by professional storytellers known as *penglipur lara*—"the soother of woes." Stories were handed down through the generations from storyteller to apprentice and were an important part of the early cultural landscape. More than entertainment, the stories and folklore served to explain the mysteries of the world and natural environment. Embedded in the stories are the beliefs, superstitions, dreams, and imaginations of the indigenous and Malay people.

The arrival of Islam in the Malay Archipelago had important significance for language and literature. The Arabic alphabet and script were introduced and adopted as the medium of writing in the Malay language. In the process, the Malay language underwent change and enrichment, borrowing a large number of Arabic and Persian words. In this way, Malay became the literary and religious lingua franca of the region, replacing the Javanese language. As the main purpose for the introduction of the Arabic script was to produce Islamic books for religious instruction, the earliest writings were religious books called *kitab* or *risalah*. In addition to being used for books on theology and philosophy, the Arabic script was subsequently used as a medium of writing for romantic and epic literature. Much of the earlier Indianized literature was Islamized and adapted into Malay.

The primary genre of prose writing was the *hikayat*, which takes its structure from the quest myth. Life experiences are intertwined with idealism, myth, imagination, and exaggeration. Numerous stories were written using this format. Examples include a Malay version of the *Ramayana* known as the *Hikayat Seri Rama* and Islamic epics such as the *Hikayat Muhammad Hanafiah*. These Islamic stories and romances were used to convey the message of Islam, instruct the people on its basic tenets, and show its values as exemplary behavior to be emulated. The most significant *hikayat* of this period was the *Sejarah Melayu* (the *Malay Annals*), claimed to represent the peak of classical Malay literature. The *Sejarah Melayu* was not a religious document but rather a historic epic consisting of royal records, genealogies, and origin myths. It remains the only available account of the history of the Malacca Sultanate in the 15th and early 16th centuries, and it covers the origins, evolution, and demise of the Sultanate, its unique system of government, administration, and politics. It also includes origin myths that have been used to explain the discovery and naming of Singapore and Malacca. Given its historical significance, the *Sejarah Melayu* was added by UNESCO to the Memory of the World International Register in 2001 in recognition of its importance to the world's literary heritage.

Alongside the *Sejarah Melayu,* the *Hikayat Hang Tuah* is regarded as a national epic in Malaysia. This document records the adventures of Hang Tuah, a great Malay warrior in the 15th century during the reign of Sultan Mansur Shah. He was popular among the people because of his bravery and good looks, yet these drew envy from several quarters. He was framed for treason, and the sultan ordered him to be executed. But, instead of executing him, the Bendahara (chief minister) sent Hang Tuah into hiding. Unaware of this turn of events, Hang Tuah's friend, Hang Jebat, rebelled against the sultan to protest the injustice of Hang Tuah's alleged execution and ran amok in the palace, causing much harm and destruction. The sultan then regretted his actions against Hang Tuah. On seeing the sultan's remorse, the Bendahara revealed that Hang Tuah was still alive. The sultan then summoned Hang Tuah to subdue Hang Jebat, and an epic battle between the two warriors ensued. While Hang Tuah was touched by his friend's loyalty, his ultimate allegiance was to the sultan. Hang Tuah eventually prevailed and killed Hang Jebat. Hang Tuah is revered as the hero for his unwavering loyalty to the ruler and has become a symbol of Malay loyalty toward the ruler and, by extension, the nation.

This rich literary tradition continues to be influential in Singapore and Malaysia. The myths and legends are retold in books and film and on television. The Hang Tuah stories have been recounted numerous times in books, comics, and films such as *Hang Tuah* (1955) and *Puteri Gunung Ledang* (2004). The story of Sang Nila Utama from the *Sejarah Melayu* still appears in the social studies and history textbooks used in Singapore schools.

MODERN LITERATURE

A pioneer in the field of modern literature was the 19th-century writer Munshi Abdullah, considered to be the father of modern Malay literature. He was perhaps the first Malay writer to depart from traditional literary styles. His seminal work, the *Hikayat Abdullah,* was an autobiography in which Abdullah recorded his reflections on contemporary life. Abdullah's work pioneered a modern perspective on literature with its emphasis on realism and contemporary society. In addition, he was the first to adopt the role of a reflective and observant social critic.

Despite Abdullah's efforts, modern forms of literature—novels, short stories, free-verse poetry—emerged only in the 20th century. In the field of Malay literature, the novel and the short story emerged in the 1920s. This was followed in the 1930s by the modern Malay free verse known as *sajak.* Early authors were teachers and journalists whose writings were driven by political and economic development as well as by social issues. In the postwar period,

Malay novels tended to dwell on the war experiences and the nationalistic fight against the Malayan Union. A number of Malay writers also felt that literature should be used to help develop nationalism and to push Malaya toward independence. To this end, ASAS 50 (*Angkatan Sasterawan* 50), a Malay literary society, was formed on August 6, 1950. The founding members of ASAS 50 have played a critical role in the development of modern Malay literature. They include Malay literary pioneers such as S. N. Masuri, an author and accomplished poet. He wrote more than 1,000 poems in his lifetime, and his works addressed issues of tradition, social justice, and spirituality in a modern setting.

Prior to 1965, Singapore was the center of Malay literature because of the concentration of newspapers and publishers in the city. However, with its separation from Malaysia, in 1965, the center shifted to Kuala Lumpur, along with a number of prominent writers. Social and political developments such as the Islamic resurgence in the 1970s and 1980s and the effects of the corporate world and technology in the 1990s were prominent themes. In 1979, the Malaysian government established a national literary award, the *Anugerah Sestera Negara,* for outstanding works by Malaysians in Malay. Its recipients include A. Samad Said (1985), best known for his novel *Salina,* which introduced realism into Malay literature, and S. Othman Kelantan (2003), a former teacher whose stories revolve around moral issues related to the poor.

Local forms of Chinese literature also emerged in the 20th century. Known as *xin ma wen xue* (Singapore-Malaysia literature), this body of work emerged as the Chinese began to identify more with the interests and aspirations of Malaya than with those of their homeland, China. The stories were set in Malaya, or Nanyang (South Seas), as it was known by the Chinese, and dealt with local themes. This localized Chinese literature was supported by the Chinese newspapers, which, in the 1920s and 1930s, called for literature with a Nanyang flavor, separate from the literature of mainland China. Literary supplements of newspapers, such as the *Wenyi zhoukan* (*Literary Weekly*) of the *Nanyang Siang Pao* in Singapore and *Ku Dao* (*Deserted Island*) of the *Yiqun Ribao* (*Yiqun Daily*) in Kuala Lumpur, were avenues for the publication of these works. Most writers used the genres of the short story and poetry to write about the issues facing the local Chinese community.

Chinese literature was very much a reflection of the times, as writers believed that literature should explore the problems and conflicts of society. During the economic depression of the 1930s, short stories such as *Ku* (*Bitterness*) and *Yi Ge Chefu De Meng* (*The Dream of a Rickshaw Puller*) dealt with the difficult lives led by the Chinese under colonial rule. Stories written in the late 1930s and 1950s were also influenced by the experience of war, particularly the Sino-Japanese war. In the postwar period, Chinese literature began to expand to a variety of subjects and to reach out to larger audiences. Well-known Chinese writers include Teo Huat (Nian Hong) a prolific writer of short stories and children's books whose works have been published in Singapore, Malaysia, Hong Kong, and Taiwan. One of Singapore's most popular Chinese writers today is Liang Wern Fook, who writes essays, short stories, poetry, novellas, and Chinese pop songs with a distinctive Singapore flavor.

Although a relatively small community, the Indians maintained a thriving Tamil literary scene. Like the Chinese, they favored the short-story form. Since the 1930s, stories have been published as compilations or in journals and magazines. Given their popularity, short stories were used as a tool of education as well as an evangelical medium for various religious groups, including the Hindus, Muslims, and Christians. As in other ethnic literatures, works by Indian authors focused on issues facing the Indian community, such as life in the rubber estates, and on national events such as the Japanese Occupation. Literary works—stories and poetry—received active support from the newspapers *Tamil Nesan* and *Tamil Murasu,* which printed and promoted them. Prominent Tamil writers include Na Govindasamy, who initiated *Ilakkiya Kalam* (literary critics' circle) in 1977 to gather the best short stories of the period, and N. Palanivelu, a novelist, playwright, and poet who wrote 50 stories between 1935 and 1960.

ENGLISH LITERATURE

Since English was introduced as the language of government, commerce, and education in the colonial period, the language has evolved from being a functional language to one in which Singaporeans and Malaysians feel comfortable expressing themselves. The growth of local English literature stemmed from tertiary institutions such as the University of Malaya, founded in 1949. University literary groups and journals such as *The Cauldron* provided writers and poets their first opportunity for publication, and writers came mainly from academic ranks. Poetry was a dominant mode in this early period. Singapore's unofficial poet laureate is Edwin Thumboo because of his nationalistic poems. Besides writing poetry, Thumboo was also responsible for many anthologies of fiction and poetry and has been a strong champion of the arts. He is professor emeritus at the National University of Singapore, the longest serving dean of the Faculty of Arts, and the first Singapore cultural medallion winner in literature (he won in 1980).

Short stories are also popular. One of Singapore's most popular short story writers is Catherine Lim, well known for her stories about Singapore society and traditional Chinese culture. Two of her early short-story compilations, *Little Ironies: Stories of Singapore* (1978) and *Or Else, The Lightning God and Other Stories,* have become bestsellers and are used as literature texts in local schools. She has since gone on to write full-length novels. One of Malaysia's leading English-language novelists was Lloyd Fernando, a former professor of English at the University of Malaya. Although not prolific, he wrote two novels, *Scorpion Orchid* (1976) and *Green Is the Colour* (1993), that are regarded as influential texts and are used in university courses. Both novels deal with the impact of nationalistic fervor and racial tensions in Singapore and Malaysia in the 1950s and 1960s. The potential of Singapore and Malaysian English writers is highlighted by the achievement of Malaysian writer Tan Twan Eng whose book *The Gift of Rain,* set in Penang during the Japanese Occupation, was long-listed for the Man Booker Prize in 2007.

TRADITIONAL ARTS AND CRAFTS

Traditional arts and crafts have been part of local culture for centuries. Their earliest forms are prehistoric paintings found in caves that illustrate the creativity of the early people of the region. The cave drawings in Sabah's Balambagan Cave have been dated between 8,000 to 10,000 years ago. Craftwork has long been essential for utilitarian as well as ceremonial purposes. Initially, handicrafts were produced to fulfill everyday needs: to provide kitchen utensils, fishing nets, farming equipment, and clothes for everyday and ceremonial wear. Rulers and chiefs employed master craftsmen to make rich fabrics and to produce other items for personal use or gifts. Although many of these items are mass-produced in factories today, these traditional crafts are still practiced in various parts of Malaysia, particularly in Sabah, Sarawak, Kelantan, and Terengganu.

The number of traditional artisans is declining rapidly. In order to stem the decline, the Malaysian government, through the Malaysian Handicraft Development Corporation (*Kraftangan*), has taken an active role in preserving these traditional skills. In addition to honoring master craftsmen and recording their work through publications and videos, it has also initiated an apprenticeship program through which young people are attached to these craftsmen to learn their skills. It also has schemes to encourage handicraft entrepreneurs by providing guidance, materials, equipment, and promotion opportunities for them. So far, the agency has experienced some success in creating several model communities where traditional crafts have been revitalized and are produced for commercial retail. At the same time, it also promotes the use of traditional crafts by the government by encouraging officials to wear clothes made from traditional textiles.

Textile Weaving

Ikat

The Malaysian indigenous tribes are adept weavers, although styles of weaving, patterns, and motifs differ from tribe to tribe. In Sarawak, the Ibans are well known for their finely crafted warp *ikat*. These are woven on simple body-tension looms from homegrown cotton colored with natural dyes prepared from the plants of the jungle. The motifs on the *ikat* are drawn from the immediate environment, such as birds, deer, and insects, and serve as a visual record of tribal beliefs and values. The most impressive of the Iban textiles is the *pua kumbu,* or "grand blanket," which measures up to 8.2 feet by 3.9 feet. It is made from two identical pieces of cloth tied together during dyeing; they form the upper and lower webs of the loom during weaving. The *pua* are decorated with numerous motifs to form complex patterns, which are combined with border patterns at the end.

Traditionally the weaving of the *pua kumbu* was regarded as a sacred activity that every Iban woman had to undertake to establish her womanhood and her place in society. It was believed that every *pua kumbu* contained a spirit that generated a supernatural force imbuing the cloth with spiritual potency. In the past, *pua kumbu* were used to receive freshly smoked head trophies from their warrior husbands on their return from successful war expeditions. The power of the blanket was said to counteract any malevolence flowing from the trophies. The *pua* were also used to define sacred spaces at ceremonies, marriage feasts, funerals, ritual purifications, and healings. In addition to its use as a spiritual tool, the *pua* embodied and reflected the social structures and the religious beliefs of the Iban people. With their conversion to Christianity and their adoption of modern ways, they no longer have a fervent belief in the spiritual powers of the *pua*. In addition, most of the younger Iban women no longer feel the need to weave these textiles, or, if they do, they tend to quickly produce inferior materials for the tourist market. Despite this trend, traditional textiles continue to be a source of pride and are still worn during festivals and weddings.

Kain Songket

The *kain songket* is considered the traditional fabric of the Malay people. It is a handwoven piece of brocaded fabric with a base of either cotton, polyester, or silk into which gold or silver threads are woven to make elaborate designs. At one time, court artisans wove the *songket* exclusively for royal use. Now it is widely used to make ceremonial attire for weddings and official functions. High-quality *songket* pieces are highly treasured and kept as family heirlooms to be handed down through the generations.

The *songket* is traditionally woven by women on a Malay floor loom called a *kek tenun* that is approximately 7.8 feet by 3.2 feet. Silk and cotton yarn are used singly or in combination for the warp and weft of the fabric, while gold and silver threads are used for the supplementary weft patterns. To emphasize the richness of the gold thread, maroon, yellow, green, brown, and blue are used as background colors. Traditional *songket* patterns are derived from the local flora and fauna such as flowers, birds, and butterflies. Motifs of food and cultural objects such as the *kris* are often incorporated into the design. *Songket* weaving is laborious and time consuming. Preparing the materials and the loom for weaving alone takes several days. It takes a weaver working about six to eight hours a day a month to complete a *sarong* measuring 3.2 feet by 5.9 feet.

The centers of traditional *songket* weaving are in Kelantan and Terengganu, where it is a cottage industry. An entrepreneur who serves as a trader runs each weaving center, collecting orders and distributing dyed yarns, beaters, and shuttles to the weavers. The weavers usually complete the fabric on their home looms in between taking care of their household responsibilities. On completing a length of fabric, the weaver returns it to the entrepreneur, who gives her a cash payment based on the length of the cloth, the workmanship, and the intricacy of the design. Although it is laborious work, the *songket* industry is relatively healthy because of the constant demand for these exquisite but expensive fabrics.

Batik

Batik is a technique for decorating textiles in which molten wax is used to cover parts of the textile that are not to be colored. Although *batik* has been around the region since the 16th century, the people of Malaya began experimenting with it only in the early 1900s. There are two main types of *batik* created in Malaysia today—block printed and handpainted *batik*. In block printing, a metal block made by welding together strips of metal is dipped into molten wax and pressed against the fabric to make the pattern. The cloth is then dyed in various colors. This is the method favored in Indonesia. In handpainted *batik*, a *canting*—a small copper container with one or more differently sized pipes—filled with molten wax is used to trace the outlines of the pattern on the fabric. Colors are then handpainted onto the fabric with the craftsperson creating shades and dimension by expertly mixing and blending colors. Applying colors this way is known as *conteng* (doodling). This form of handpainted *batik* emerged in the late 20th century as a distinct Malaysian innovation. It simplifies the Javanese *batik* tradition, opening it up to greater individuality and creativity. *Batik* is used to make the popular *baju kurongs* and *batik* shirts, which are often worn at formal occasions.

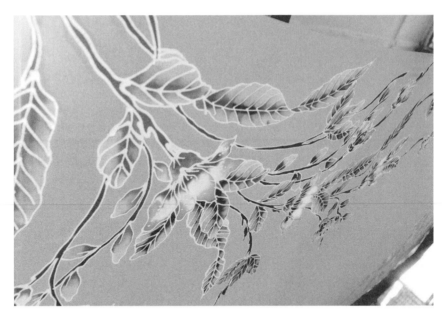

Handpainted *batik* is a distinct Malaysian innovation and used widely to make *baju kurongs* and *batik* shirts. Courtesy of the author.

Woodcarving

Given that Malaysia has huge tracts of rain forests with an abundant supply of wood, it is no wonder that woodcarving is one of the most widely practiced crafts. Woodcarving was an important part of domestic and formal Malay life. Carved household items such as biscuit molds and coconut scrapers were essential parts of the kitchen. Wooden panels are also de rigueur for traditional Malay homes. Woodcarvers constructed walls and partitions that fulfilled practical functions such as creating enclosed spaces in the home. There are two main kinds of panels: the low relief, which allows for intricate patterns, and the cut-out, which admits greater amounts of air. Woodcarving is also an integral component of grander structures such as mosques and palaces. For example, the *mimbar* (pulpit) in a mosque is made up of elaborate and detailed woodcarving work that enables it to serve as the focal point for mosque's interior. Woodcarving is also used extensively in traditional palaces in the roofs, walls, pillars, and doorways to convey the grandeur of the structure. As in the other crafts, the motifs used in woodcarving reflect the changing influences in Malaysia. Early motifs had Hindu-Buddhist origins and often depicted mythical gods; these motifs were later transformed into abstract or natural forms to reflect the Islamic ethos.

Woodcarving is an integral part of the Malay culture. It is used extensively in homes, palaces, and mosques as decorations or as part of the structural design. Courtesy of the author.

Gold, Silver, and Pewter Work

Peninsular Malaysia was once known as the Golden Chersonese because of the richness of its gold deposits. However, the fashioning of gold ornaments owed much to the patronage of the Malay royalty, who wore gold jewelry during official functions and ceremonies. An important item of the ceremonial dress was the *pending* (belt buckle), often encrusted with precious gems. Traditional Malay goldsmiths were particularly skillful in repoussé (the art of embossing a pattern in relief onto a thin sheet of gold) and granulation (the process of applying tiny grains of molten gold onto the surface of an ornament). The granules were decorative and helped to secure individual pieces of gold in place, particularly when an ornament comprised several segments, embossed separately and then cut and soldered together. Other communities, such as the Chinese and the Indians, who share a fondness for gold jewelry, also adopted the ornamentation styles used by the Malay goldsmiths. The Chinese goldsmiths used these styles to create the gold *kerosang*, sets of three identical or matching brooches for the Peranakan women.

Although silver is not indigenous to the region, silversmithing developed into a craft from Malaysia. The indigenous Malay craftsmen worked under royal patronage and created receptacles such as betel nut sets, bowls, and trays for royal weddings and daily use. They also created jewelry such as pendants, hairpins, and tiaras. The Chinese craftsmen fashioned jewelry, bed ornaments, and hospitality and ritual items mainly for the wealthy Peranakan families. Instead of the Malay floral patterns, these craftsmen used traditional Chinese motifs such as the peony, pomegranate, crane, and deer. These were also used in elaborate wedding ceremonies.

In the late 19th century, Malaya was one of the world's largest producers of tin. Its rich tin deposits attracted many Chinese migrants to work in the tin mines or as tinsmiths. One of these migrants, Yong Koon, was a pewtersmith who began to craft domestic items such as teapots, kettles, jugs, and religious altarpieces out of pewter, a metal alloy of tin and lead. In the early days, pewter making was laborious, because the metal had to be heated and cast into sheets before being knocked into shape with a wooden mallet, filed, and polished. Over time, Yong Koon and his family expanded their range of pewter products in order to cater to British and foreign markets. They also modernized their production process with the use of molds that allowed them to cast the pewter into a wider range of shapes. His company became known as Selangor Pewter. In 1979, the company received a royal warrant from the Sultan of Selangor and has since become known as Royal Selangor. It is now the largest maker of pewter objects in the world and has even expanded into gold and silver work.

Kris

The *kris* (or *keris*) is a short-bladed weapon that has been used by the Malays for more than 600 years. It is regarded as the national weapon of the Malays and remains an object of mystery, believed to possess spiritual power to protect its owner from physical harm and misfortune. Traditionally used as a weapon of self-defense, the *kris* is still part of the Malay royal regalia but is now retained more for decorative than for practical usage. The *kris* is still made by traditional Malay craftsmen. The blade made by the ironsmith—*pandai besi* (artist-craftman in iron)—is usually 12 to 15 inches long and can be straight or wavy. The wavy edges are created by repeatedly reheating the metal and hammering the edges against the side of the anvil. The waves or curves are referred to as *lok* and are always odd in number varying from 5 to 47 in a single blade. The blades are also distinguished by a *pamur* or damasked finishing created by using a hammer to work nickel into the iron blade. The Malays believe that a good *kris* should contain at least two or more types of iron, because inclusion of different metals is believed to strengthen the blade.

A woodcarver usually makes the hilt and the sheath of the *kris* using wood with an ornamental grain. The hilt is about 4 to 5 inches long and is typically bent at about the middle of its length to provide a pistol grip. In the pre-Islamic era, hilts were carved in the form of Hindu-Buddhist or animist gods, heroes, or demons. These designs were later replaced by more abstract floral and geometric designs that were acceptable to Islam. The sheath is usually not carved and consists of three parts: the broad crosspiece, which rests at the head of the shaft; the body, which is straight and of uniform width; and the tip, which may be reinforced with a thin strip of ivory or iron. The most beautiful hilts and sheaths found in the royal regalia are often made of gold and silver engraved in traditional patterns.

Kitemaking (*Wau*)

Making the Malaysian kite (*wau*) is a traditional craft that is still alive in the northern states of Malaysia. These handmade kites usually measure 3 to 5 feet long and come in various shapes that are intricately decorated with layers of colored paper, resulting in a stained-glass effect. A bow on the head of the kite makes a humming noise when it is flown. Depending on the size, kite makers can take from one week to a month to make a kite. The frame of the kite is made from bamboo stems split into thin strips and then bent and tied into shapes. The most popular shapes are that of the moon (*wau bulan*) or those inspired by animals such as the peacock, cat, and fish. After the frame is

Traditional handcrafted kites on display in a craftsman's workroom. Courtesy of the author.

shaped, it is covered with tinted, glazed paper. Designs, predominantly leaves and flowers, are traced on shiny foil paper and then cut out with a sharp penknife. These cut-outs are glued onto the glazed paper using rice paste. A humming bow made of a thin strip of ribbon is attached to the head of the kite, and tassels are added to the tail. Many of these kites are flown during the annual kite festival in Kelantan (mentioned in Chapter 8) or at international kite competitions. In many instances, these beautiful kites have become items for home decoration.

MODERN VISUAL ARTS

The British colonialists introduced Western visual arts to Malaya in the 19th century. The early British administrators documented their new environment through botanical drawings, landscape paintings, and watercolors, and this early works exposed the locals to the romantic and detailed style of Western art. Pioneers of modern Malaysian art were the Penang watercolorists who were active around the 1930s. Their paintings, in a naturalistic style that focused on nature and daily life, were a radical departure from traditional art and crafts, which were generally abstract and symbolic. Their use of watercolor, which is well suited to outdoor painting, introduced a new artistic medium to the region.

The next significant art movement came as a result of émigré artists from China who settled in Singapore. Their fusion of Western and Eastern approaches, combined with the use of the local environment as subject matter, resulted in the creation of a "Nanyang" style of art. The movement is associated with the Nanyang Academy of Fine Arts (NAFA), established in Singapore in 1937, the only art institution in Southeast Asia at that time. Founded by Lim Hak Tai, an artist from Foochow trained in Chinese and Western art techniques, the school was the first to introduce Western approaches to art such as impressionism, post-impressionism, fauvism, and cubism. Most Nanyang artists such as Cheong Soo Pieng and Georgette Chen taught in NAFA at some time or the other. Although differing in style, the Nanyang artists were joined by a common interest to "integrate the cultures of the different races; bridge the arts of the East and West; promote the scientific spirit and social conscience; create an art form typical of our tropical nation; nurture creative talent."[2]

The Nanyang artists focused on depicting the local environment through their landscape, portrait, and still-life paintings. They focused on scenes of daily life, and used settings such as villages, religious buildings and markets, depicting everyday objects and local fruits. The artists, however, experimented with different Western styles. Georgette Chen, who had lived and worked in

Paris before coming to Singapore, was heavily influenced by Cezanne and Van Gogh, and this was reflected in her paintings. Cheong Soo Pieng, on the other hand, was influenced by Cubism and often painted in a highly stylized manner that can be compared to the works of Picasso, as well as to comics and cartoons.

One of the most important art groups in Malaysia was the Angkatan Pelukis Semenanjung (APS), now known as the Angkatan Pelukis Se-Malaysia, formed in 1956. The aim of the group was to promote art with Malaysian characteristics as the basis of national art. Similar to the Nanyang artists, APS artists concentrated on portraits and landscapes of local scenes and people using traditional artistic and cultural motifs; however, they painted in a strongly naturalistic style. This was in part a reflection of the strong influence of Hoessein Enas, a Javanese artist who migrated to Malaya after the Second World War and who was the main coordinator of the group. His expertise was in figurative realism, and he painted a wide range of portraits depicting Malayan people and culture. The group also played an important role in improving art education and awareness by organizing art and music classes as well as exhibitions.

Since the postwar years, artists from Singapore and Malaysia have gone to Europe and to the United States for travel and studies and have brought back new approaches and techniques to art. Universal movements such as expressionism and abstract expressionism have thus influenced the work of local artists. At the time, art has also been influenced by the political and social issues of the day. In Singapore, the 1950s and 1960s were a period of great political upheavals, and art in the form of woodblock prints and paintings in the social realist genre were used to support the nationalist cause. In the 1970s and 1980s, artists became concerned with a search for national identity and culture, especially in Malaysia, because of the launch of the National Culture policy in 1971. In their search for a Malaysian art, artists began to look to traditional art forms as well as Islamic art as sources of inspiration. The appearance of traditional motifs and art forms such as *batik*, shadow puppets, and traditional Malay houses became more apparent during this period. In some cases, artists also incorporated Islamic calligraphy or geometric shapes into their work.

In addition to painting, artists began to experiment with sculpture and mixed media by the 1960s. As a medium devoted to the expression of an idea, aesthetic, or concern without a spiritual or religious meaning, this art form is relatively new to the region. One of Singapore's most prominent sculptors was Ng Eng Teng who created more than 300 sculptures over his lifetime. His sculpture *Mother and Child* (1980) is a major piece of public art located on the grounds of the National University of Singapore. One of Malaysia's earliest modern sculptors was Anthony Lau, who used materials such as concrete, wood, and metal in order to demonstrate their unique qualities. A representative work is *Spirit of Fire* (1960), which evokes the mystical essence of fire through vertical flame-like woodcarving.

By the 1980s and 1990s, art in Singapore and Malaysia expanded into a diversity of styles and media derived from aesthetic concepts of Western, Asian, and Islamic traditions. Some of the contemporary art forms that have gained a following are installation, performance, and digital art, as well as photography. There have emerged many young artists who continue to push the boundaries of art. Contemporary art now often uses multiple mediums, as in the work of Malaysian Wong Hoy Cheong, whose most memorable *Re: Looking,* made up of an installation work, a video, and a Web site, was displayed at the 2003 Venice Biennale. Contemporary art is likely to become more important in the future. Since 2006, Singapore has organized the Singapore Biennale, a biannual festival of contemporary visual art that has received positive reviews and helped Singapore make its mark on the international art scene. In addition, there is increasing support for contemporary art from state institutions such as the National Museum of Singapore and the Singapore Art Museum, as well as the National Art Gallery in Malaysia.

NOTES

1. Katherine Sim, *More Than a Pantun: Understanding Malay Verse* (Singapore, Times Books International, 1987), p. 12.

2. Quoted in Suzie Koay, "Singapore: Multi-cultural Crossroads," in Haji Abdul Ghani Haji Bujang et al., *Visual Arts in ASEAN: Continuity and Change* (Kuala Lumpur: Association of Southeast Asian Nations Committee on Culture and Information, 2001), p. 169.

SUGGESTED READINGS

Asmah Haji Oman (ed.). *The Encyclopedia of Malaysia, Vol. 9: Languages and Literature.* Singapore: Editions Didier Millet, 2004.

Haji Abdul Ghani Haji Bujang et al. *Visual Arts in ASEAN: Continuity and Change.* Kuala Lumpur: Association of Southeast Asian Nations Committee on Culture and Information, 2001.

Hasnah Haji Ibrahim (ed.). *Anthology of ASEAN Literatures, Malaysia: Indigenous Traditions.* Kuala Lumpur: ASEAN Committee on Culture and Information, 1985.

Kwok, Kian Chow. *Channels & Confluences: A History of Singapore Art.* Singapore: Singapore Art Museum, 1996.

Syed Ahmad Jamal (ed.). *The Encyclopedia of Malaysia, Vol. 14: Crafts and the Visual World.* Singapore: Editions Didier Millet, 2007.

4

Performing Arts and Entertainment

PERFORMING ARTS AND entertainment in Singapore and Malaysia are typified by diversity more than anything else. Traditionally, each ethnic group has its own particular form of performing arts. Dance, drama, and music were part of the groups' spiritual rituals, ceremonies and celebrations, and are important sources of identity. The Westernization of Singapore and Malaysian societies have led to the introduction of newer performance types and entertainment media whose popularity and practices often cut across ethnic boundaries. Western performing arts, both high-brow and popular, have become critical parts of the local cultural scene. Elite Western performing arts such as ballet, symphonic music, and theater have a strong following among the educated classes, while the appeal of popular entertainment—radio, television, and film— cuts across all ethnic groups and classes. Young Singaporeans and Malaysians especially show a preference for Western-influenced entertainment; they listen to American Top 40 pop songs, do hip-hop and break dancing, and flock to the cinemas to watch Hollywood blockbusters. This chapter highlights the myriad traditional and contemporary performing arts and entertainment in the Singapore and Malaysian cultural landscape.

TRADITIONAL DANCE, MUSIC, AND THEATER

Traditional dance, music, and theater were critical elements of spiritual and healing rituals practiced by the indigenous and Malay communities.

With increased influence of Christianity, Islam, and Western education, these performances are now staged more often as entertainment than for their spiritual significance. Although traditional dance and music are still a part of local weddings and celebrations, more often than not they are now performed in formal arenas such as the Sarawak Cultural Village or the Istana Budaya, Kuala Lumpur's center for the arts. Such traditional performing arts are now considered main attractions for cultural and heritage tourism.

Indigenous Arts

Among the indigenous tribes, there has customarily been little separation of dance, music, and theater. Performances were associated with rituals and combined elements of dance, music, and drama with a state of trance. Many tribes believed that diseases were caused by malevolent spirits, and thus illness could be cured by healing theater or performances to appease these spirits. During these performances, a shaman would make contact with the offending spirits and negotiate with them or compel them to leave the sick person, thus healing him.

In Sabah, one of the most well-known dances is the *sumazau,* performed by the Kadazan communities in the Panampang and Papar areas. This dance is performed for both ritual and celebratory purposes: to call upon or placate spirits, to exorcise spirits from newly built houses, and to celebrate occasions such as thanksgiving (*manginakan*), moving to a new house (*magang*), the blooming of padi shoots (*monogit*), or to pay homage to padi spirits (*humabot*). The dance is typically performed by pairs of men and women in tribal costumes of black cloth decorated with locally-made gold braid. The basic movements consist of dancers shifting their weight from one foot to the other while swinging their arms in time to the music. These movements are done with bent knees or on tiptoe and are accompanied by music produced by a hanging gong ensemble.

The Ibans of Sarawak believe that dreams are omens and that particular birds are guardians and gods. These augural birds are honored during ritual festivals through dance and music. The Iban term for dance is *ngajat,* and the fundamental dance movements imitate the movements of birds. Typical dance gestures include the *burung terbang* (bird flying), in which the dancer, with outstretched arms, bends the torso and crosses the feet like a bird sweeping high in the sky, and the *titi papan* and *titi tiong,* in which the dancer makes a sidestepping motion of the feet while bending and folding the arms and rotating the wrists. The *ngajat bebhunuh* is a lively dance in which two Iban warriors duel with each other. The warrior-dancers wear elaborate headgear adorned with long silvery features of pheasants and hornbills. Armed with machetes and shields, the dancers try to outsmart their opponent by

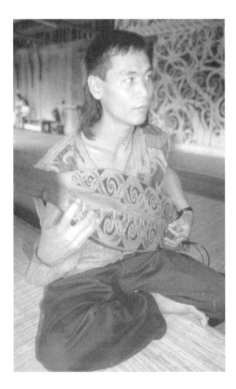

A tribesman in Sarawak playing the *sape*. Courtesy of the author.

executing fast but delicate movements accentuated by battle cries. A *sape* and *jatung utang* ensemble provides the musical accompaniment. The *sape* is a plucked lute with a long body and a short neck; it resembles a guitar. The *jatung utang* is a xylophone of wooden keys tuned to specific scales. Wooden beaters are used to strike the keys.

Malay Arts

The rich tradition of Malay dance, music, and theater falls into two main categories: court performances originating from the palaces of the Malay sultans and folk performances and theater that derive from the villages. The northern Malaysian states of Kelantan and Terengganu were traditional strongholds of traditional Malay performing arts. In recent years, however, these states have come under the control of a fundamentalist Islamic political party, Pan Malaysian Islamic Party (PAS), which has banned many traditional performances on the basis that they are un-Islamic because they are based on Hindu epics and that they promote superstition. Furthermore, interest in traditional performances is declining, and there are few young people interested in learning these arts. Nevertheless, universities and the government play an important role in preserving these performing traditions. Tertiary institutions such as the Universiti Sains Malaysia (USM), Pulau Pinang, and the Akademi Seni Kebangsaan (ASK) Malaysia in Kuala Lumpur are documenting, teaching, and performing these art forms in order to perpetuate them. The Malaysian government also supports these forms by conferring awards to exemplary traditional artists. In 1993, the *wayang kulit* puppeteer Hamzah Awang Amat from Kelantan was awarded the first *Anugerah Seni Negara* (National Arts Award).

Court dances and theater were entertainment for nobility, especially during special occasions such as birthdays and weddings of royalty and the arrival of foreign visitors. Traditional court dances include the *asyik,* a seated dance that depicts court maidens grooming themselves or mimicking the stylized gestures of birds in flight; the *joget gamelan,* a fast-paced dance accompanied by a *gamelan,* a musical ensemble consisting of a variety of instruments such as metallophones, xylophones, drums, and gongs; and the *mak yong,* which is, more accurately, a form of dance theater. The *mak yong* was initially performed as part of a shamanic trance ritual (*main puteri*) but subsequently came under royal patronage and was elevated to the status of a performing art. The content and presentation of the *mak yong* also came to revolve around mythological themes and the intrigues of royalty. Based on a limited number of stories, the plays had no written scripts, and the dialogue was improvised. Although few stage props were used, costumes were elaborate and the acting highly stylized.

Village performances came in various forms. A popular form of theater is the *wayang kulit,* which consists of stories told by a *dalang* (puppet master) who manipulates the parchment puppets seen in shadows projected onto a screen. The *dalang* controls the puppets, recites the stories, which are usually taken from the Ramayana or *Hikayat Seri Rama,* and sings songs. There are many puppet characters, each with its own distinctive traits and voice, and the *dalang* has to be highly skilled to convincingly play the various characters. A musical ensemble that includes a flute, drums, and gongs accompanies him. Performances often carry over several nights in order for an entire tale to be told. There are various types of *wayang kulit* styles, but one of the most popular and widespread is the *wayang kulit kelantan* or *wayang kulit siam,* which is performed in the northern states of Kelantan, Terengganu, and Kedah. Similar forms of shadow puppetry are also performed in Indonesia and Thailand.

Music and dance were also popular and integral parts of traditional celebrations and ceremonies. In the early 19th century, the *ronggeng,* a performance of song and dance, was frequently staged to celebrate successful harvests and the important life milestones such as weddings or the birth of children. In the *ronggeng, pantuns* (Malay quatrains) were sung in repartee accompanied

A shadow puppet used in the traditional Wayang Kulit. Courtesy of the author.

by a violin, an accordion, a *rebana,* and a gong. In addition, traditional folk dances such as the *asli,* a dance characterized by the graceful curling and flexing of fingers; the *inang,* a slower dance where dancers rhythmically pace around in circles; and the *joget,* a fast-paced dance that resembles the Malaccan-Portuguese dance known as the *brango,* were performed. Another form of sung entertainment popular at weddings and celebrations is the *dikir barat,* which features the singing of four-line *pantuns* in response style between a soloist singer and a chorus.

The *bangsawan,* which emerged as a popular form of theater in the early 20th century, was brought to the region by way of touring Parsi troupes. It is now regarded as a transitional theater that bridged the gap between the traditional and the modern. Like its theatrical predecessors, the *bangsawan* is a dramatic performance with drama, dance, song, and music. A critical element that set it apart from earlier theater was its commercial basis; the *bangsawan* was performed for entertainment and not as part of rituals or ceremonies. Its stories were derived from varied sources such as classical tales from the Middle East, India, the Malay Archipelago, and even the West. Even Shakespearean plays such as *Hamlet* and *The Merchant of Venice* were part of the *bangsawan* repertoire. Like traditional Malay theater, the *bangsawan* was staged without scripts. Instead, the director presented the actors with a scenario or story summary, and the actors improvised dialogues and song lyrics accordingly. The quality of the performance was thus highly dependent on the skill and talent of the actors. This resulted in a "star system" where the prima donna and the male lead were widely adored and well paid. The 1920s and 1930s were the heyday of the *bangsawan,* with several professional troupes actively touring Malaya and Singapore. Its popularity declined after the Second World War, mainly because of the new fascination with movies and television.

Chinese Arts

When they emigrated to Singapore and Malaya, the Chinese brought along their rich dance and theater traditions. Although interest in the arts was not high in the pioneering days, the various Chinese associations ensured that traditional performances, such as the lion dance, were maintained because they were critical components of festive celebrations. The lion dance, particularly the *cai qing,* is performed during Chinese New Year festivities and during the opening of new shops. The highlight of this dance is the lion, which is brought to life by two dancers, one manipulating the colorful papier mache lion's head and the other operating its cloth body at the rear. The dance is performed to the resounding beat of a barrel drum and cymbals. During the *cai qing,* a prize of vegetables and a red packet of money are hung from a high place. In a test of their skill, the lion dancers have to make various leaps in order to pluck or capture the prize.

Apart from the lion dance, one of the most popular traditional entertainments is the Chinese street opera. Although there are different styles of opera performed in different Chinese dialects—for example, there are Cantonese, Teochew, Hokkian, and Beijing operas, to name just a few—they all share similar features. The operas are based on traditional Chinese classics such as *Romance of the Three Kingdoms, The Water Margin,* and *Madam White Snake.* The operas integrate acting, singing, and acrobatics, with the actors wearing extremely elaborate and expressive costumes and makeup. Two main features of opera that help the audience differentiate among the characters are the acting and the makeup. The personalities of the characters are revealed through actions such as the manner of walking and hand gestures. In Chinese opera, even minor aspects assume great theatrical significance; for example, the way characters manipulate the very long and loose "water sleeves" can demonstrate whether they are angry, shy, or sad.

The identity, status, and personality of the characters are also reflected in their makeup. Brows, eyelids, and jowls painted in various patterns and shape represent different sentiments. Colors play an important role in opera makeup. In the case of the Peking Opera (opera sung in standard Mandarin), for example, white usually symbolizes wickedness and viciousness, while black represents selflessness and justice. The opera is accompanied by a musical ensemble of Chinese instruments comprising wind instruments such as the flute (*dizi*) and the double reed oboe (*suona*), string instruments such as the *erhu* and *sanxian,* and percussion instruments such as gongs, cymbals, clappers, and bells.

Chinese operas were first staged as part of religious rituals for the Chinese deities. In the past and even today, temples and associations fund these performances to glorify deities or to appease the souls of the dead during Chinese festivals such as the Hungry Ghost Festival. Over time, local professional troupes were formed, and Chinese opera has won appreciation as an art form, not just as part of a religious ceremony. With the greater appreciation of Chinese opera have come a number of troupes that now perform in permanent theaters and continue to attract a healthy audience. In Singapore, there have been attempts to broaden the appeal of Chinese opera by including English subtitles and even experimenting with singing the opera in English. While this allows the English educated to enjoy opera, many opera buffs prefer opera as it is traditionally sung.

Indian Arts

Indian folk dance came to the region as an integral part of the religious ceremonies, temple festivals, and marriages of the Indian community. An example is the *karagattam* (or pot dance) that is performed during the festival of the Indian goddess Mariamman. During the dance, the goddess is called into a *karagam* (earthern pot) that is balanced on the dancers' heads as they dance in a trance. The dance begins slowly before accelerating into fast, whirling movements with dancers performing acrobatics while still balancing the pots. Another popular dance performed in the temple is the *kolattam,* which is a lively dance performed by young boys dressed in *jippa* and *dhoti* with shawls tied around their waists and by girls dressed in saris and with bells around their ankles. The dancers strike pairs of sticks with their partners at cross rhythms with their feet to the beat of the drums.

Indian classical dance came to the region after World War II, introduced through visits from classically trained Indian dancers. As more classically trained dancers came to settle in Singapore, they set up dance academies such as the Indian Fine Arts Society of Singapore (1949) and Bhaskar's Academy of Dance (1952). These academies encourage interest in traditional Indian dance by bringing in teachers from India to conduct classes. Indian classical dance in the region is therefore performed very much as it is in India. In Malaysia, one of the earliest Indian dance schools was the Sivadas-Vatsa Dance Troupe, established in 1953, which trained hundreds of students. Today, the Temple of Fine Arts, established in Kuala Lumpur in 1981, is one of the most influential institutions for classical Indian dance training.

The *bharatanatyam* and the *odissi* are two of the most popular types of classical Indian dances in Singapore and Malaysia today. The *bharatanatyam* is an ancient dance that originated in South India. It was traditionally performed in the temples but is now more often performed in theaters. The dance technique is complex, comprising hundreds of steps, hand gestures, and neck and eye movements. The dance has a strong sculptural quality, with dancers punctuating the dance with *karanas* (dance postures) that can be seen in ancient sculptures in Hindu temples. These dances are accompanied by the *mridangam* (a type of drum), the *nagaswaram* (a long pipe horn made from a black wood), and stringed instruments like the *veena,* violin, and flute. The *odissi* originated in the eastern Indian state of Orissa and reflects both the lyrical and the vigorous aspects of dance. *Odissi* dancers use their head and upper body in soft flowing movements, along with hand gestures, to express specific moods and emotions. Music accompaniment is provided by the *pakhawaj* (a north Indian version of the *mridangam* drum), the flute, metal cymbals, and stringed instruments such as the *sitar* and the *tambura.*

CONTEMPORARY DANCE, THEATER, AND MUSIC

The influence of Western and modern performing culture has been strong in both Singapore and Malaysia. Elite performing arts such as classical ballet, theater, and classical music were among the first art forms to be introduced to the region. Subsequently, popular music, dance, film, and television became a part of everyday life in these two countries. Although many of the popular media are derived from foreign countries such as the United States, Europe, Hong Kong, Japan, and Korea, there have been attempts to localize these media to create a modern Singapore and Malaysia popular culture.

Music

The study of classical music and Western instruments such as the piano, organ, and violin is popular in Singapore and the urban centers of Malaysia. Music education typically follows the syllabi of the British international music examination boards, such as the Associated Board of the Royal Schools of Music and the Trinity College of Music of London. A number of talented individuals have furthered their studies abroad and have gone on to become successful professional musicians, such as the renowned Singapore violinist Siow Lee Chin. Siow made her performance debut in 1991 at the Carnegie Hall Recital Hall and won the Artists International Competition that year. Since then, she has performed extensively in the United States and Europe and with celebrated orchestras such as the Royal Philharmonic Orchestra of London.

The appreciation of Western classical music is, however, still in its nascent stages. Although there are increasing numbers of local musicians, the audience is still rather small. Singapore's only Western symphonic orchestra, the Singapore Symphony Orchestra, was formed in 1979. In the early years, most of the musicians were foreigners; today locals make up a majority of the 96 members of this professional orchestra. The foremost symphony orchestra in Malaysia is the Malaysian Philharmonic Orchestra, founded in 1997, based in Kuala Lumpur, and sponsored by the local petroleum company Petronas. The orchestra has 105 musicians from 25 countries and has made a commitment to nurturing and promoting interest in classical music in Malaysia and to encouraging local talent.

With widespread English education, more Singaporeans and Malaysians listen to popular Western music of various genres such as pop, country, rock, and ballads. In addition, these music styles have influenced local music content. In the mid-1960s, when the Beatles were taking the United States and Europe by storm, an imitative style known as *pop yeh yeh* emerged in the region. These bands usually consisted of four members who sang and played the basic four musical instruments: two electric guitars, an electric bass, and drums. The songs had simple melodies and were sung in English and Malay. These groups were locally known as *kuqiran* bands; their songs, recorded on vinyl, sold well in the region. Subsequently, Malay popular music also took on other Western styles such as soft rock, heavy metal, hip-hop, and rap.

In Singapore, Chinese popular music has the strongest following. In the 1980s, a style of Singapore songs known as *xinyao* emerged. *Xinyao* was akin to the folk music produced in Taiwan during the 1970s and in the United States in the 1960s. The singer-songwriters, often college or university students, sang of universal themes of life, family, friendship, and love. The songs were usually performed by a soloist or a group, with simple guitar accompaniments. Although *xinyao* is not as popular now as it was during the 1980s, these musical pioneers paved the way for a small but influential group of local Chinese pop singers such as Stephanie Sun, JJ Lin, and Eric Moo, who have become popular in Taiwan, Hong Kong, and China.

Although popular local music is still divided along language lines, there have been some attempts at creating a unique music that would blend the different musical traditions. A pioneer in the field is Singaporean Dick Lee, whose albums in the 1980s, such as *The Mad Chinaman* and *Orientalism,* were attempts at updating traditional folk songs (in various languages) through the synthesis and the application of newer musical styles of rap and jazz. The albums gave Lee a popular following in Singapore, Malaysia, and Japan. Lee has since written songs for a variety of genres including local musical theater, Chinese pop, and national songs commissioned by the government.

Dance

Although the British introduced ballet in the early 20th century, it became popular among the locals only in the 1950s. Aspiring dancers who wanted to further their ballet training had to go overseas because there were few resources in Singapore and Malaysia. On their return, these dancers laid the foundations for the local ballet and modern dance scene. In 1958, the Singapore Ballet Academy was formed and served as an important organization for raising the profile of Western dance and nurturing a new generation of dancers. The Academy also paved the way for the creation of Singapore's first professional dance company, the Singapore Dance Theatre (SDT), in 1987. One of Singapore's best-known dancer-choreographers was Goh Choo San, who served as resident choreographer for the Washington Ballet in the 1970s and who created acclaimed works for ballet companies around the world.

One of Malaysia's dance pioneers is Lee Lee Lan, a trained ballerina and an award-winning choreographer. Lee established one of the largest private dance schools in Southeast Asia, the Federal Academy of Ballet, in 1967, and trained a new generation of dancers, including Joseph Gonzales, who later become the head of the National Arts Academy. In 1984, she formed the Kuala Lumpur Dance Theatre to serve as the performing arm of the ballet academy. Lee has always been an innovative choreographer who attempted to fuse and synthesize different cultural dance elements in her work. An example is a full-length two-act Malay ballet, *Soraya,* which she choreographed to music by the Malaysian composer Julia Chong. The movements of the performance were based on classical ballet, but the finale of the ballet was a medley of dances from Malay, Chinese, and Indian traditional dance.

Contemporary dancers and choreographers in both Singapore and Malaysia today train locally and overseas in diverse dance traditions. There continues to be a keen interest in synthesizing different dance vocabularies and traditions in ways that are more fluid, sophisticated, and seamless than the ethnic dance medleys typical of tourist cultural performances. Some breakthroughs in this field include *AWAS!,* choreographed by Joseph Gonzales, which explored traditional Malay dance forms such as the *mak yong* and *zapin* and infused them with Western dance technique set to Asian music. Another example was *Re: Lady White Snake,* choreographed by Mew Chang Tsing and Lee Swee Keong. The performance was an adaptation and a retelling of a famous Chinese legend by blending Javanese, Balinese, Malay, Indian, Chinese, and Western dance movements that evolved through improvisation.

Alongside the formal dance institutions, dance is much a part of life for Singaporeans and Malaysians. Many children learn ballet, while ballroom, tango, salsa, jazz, and line dance are popular with well-heeled adults. There is also an active club scene, especially in Singapore, where dance clubs attract thousands on the weekend to do free-style dance to disco, trance, and house music. Hip-hop has also gained an active following among teenagers, who can be often seen on weekends in baggy pants practicing their moves in various public areas.

Theater

Although Western plays have long been staged in the region, it was only in the 1950s and 1960s that this form of theater began to influence local dramatists. In this period, local playwrights, influenced by George Bernard Shaw, Arthur Miller, and Tennessee Williams, began to create works that explored social problems set in contemporary society. This was a departure from traditional theater, which concentrated on retelling stories from a mythical past. In addition, playwrights began to write scripts for their plays instead of relying on improvisation, as was the tradition. This movement was called *drama moden* (modern drama). A seminal work in this genre was Mustapha Kamil Yassin's play *Atap Genting Atap Rembia* (*Brick House Nipa House*), which explored the clash of cultures between urban and rural values, the young and the old, the Malays and the Chinese.

Subsequently, modern Malay theater developed through various stages in which new theatrical forms such as experimental and neorealistic theater were introduced. Experimental theater allowed greater room for improvisation and interaction with the audience and had a more provocative edge. An influential experimental dramatist was Noordin Hassan, whose first work, *Bukan Lalang Di Tiup Angin* (*It Is Not Tall Grass That Is Blown by the Wind*) was a critique of the May 13, 1969, racial riots in Malaysia (see Chapter 1). Neorealism was less concerned with the concept of realism and was often scripted to closely resemble film screenplays. Examples of this technique can be found in Johan Jaafar's plays, one of which had 26 acts and used film techniques such as fade-in, fade-out, and dissolve.

Theater in Singapore has conventionally been divided along linguistic and ethnic lines. Although there are theater companies that focus on Mandarin, Malay, and Indian theater, English-language theater has seen the most growth. This is in large part a result of the widespread use of English in Singapore society and its effectiveness as a medium for interethnic communication. Even in Malaysia, where Malay theater is still dominant, English-language theater has gained in popularity. Local plays in English were first written in the 1960s by Singapore playwrights, who, like their Malaysian counterparts, wrote naturalistic plays set in the local context in imitation of British modes of dramatic structure. An influential playwright during this period was Robert Yeo, who broke ground by writing about political and social issues in his plays such as *One Year Back Home* (1980). Theater director Max Le Bond was influential in the 1980s in creating a movement to give English-language theater a Singapore face rather than just enacting plays from the British repertoire. Significantly, his direction of Stella Kon's *Emily of Emerald Hill* spotlighted Singapore in the international arena.

Although English-language theater is one of the most popular forms, the doyen of modern Singapore theater, Kuo Pao Kun, was a strong advocate for multilingual theater that would better reflect multicultural Singapore. Kuo used seven local dialects and languages for his breakthrough play, *Mama Looking for Her Cat* (1988). As a strong advocate for local arts, Kuo started the Practice Performing Arts School with his dancer wife, Goh Lay Kuan, in 1965. The school has been an important training ground for many of Singapore's current theater professionals. In 1990, Kuo founded The Substation: Home for the Arts, which became a venue and meeting place for different artistic disciplines. In 2001, with T. Sasitharan, he started the Theatre Training Research Programme, which provided training for actors and directors in four major Asian traditions—Noh Theater, Wayang Wong, Bharatanatyam, and Chinese Xi Qu. Throughout his career, Kuo was interested in merging different languages and styles of theater to form something relevant, unique, and local. This multilingual form of theater is still an ideal that many local dramatists continue to explore today.

Since the 1980s, professional theater companies have expanded significantly and now stage a range of works, from local plays to international musicals to avant-garde dramas. Singapore and Malaysia also have invested in purpose-built venues for hosting theater productions. The Esplanade in Singapore and Istana Budaya in Kuala Lumpur, Malaysia, are two such premium venues. In addition, plays are also hosted in many smaller theaters, schools, and clubhouses.

Film

Film came to the region in the early 20th century. By the 1950s, two major studios based in Singapore—Malay Film Productions, owned by the Shaw Brothers, and Cathay-Keris Productions—dominated the regional film industry, churning out an impressive number of Malay films. During this period, Singapore was the center of Malay cinema and the Hollywood of Southeast Asia.[1] With a few exceptions, most films produced during this period were in Malay and were created for audiences in Singapore, Malaysia, and Indonesia. The early films were heavily influenced by the traditional *bangsawan* in terms of cast and repertoire. Not only were *bangsawan* actors recruited, but their repertoire of local historical stories, local folktales, and a mixture of Arabian, Indian, Chinese, and even European classics formed the basis of most films.

One of the biggest stars of the era was the multitalented singer, actor, director, playwright, and producer P. Ramlee. Ramlee was initially picked out for his singing ability rather than for his looks; he was often cast as the ubiquitous villain. His composing and performing skills eventually made him popular, and he went on to star in films such as *Bakti* (*Faithfulness*) and *Penghidupan* (*Life*) that catapulted him to stardom. Ramlee made his directorial debut with *Penarek Becha* (*Trishaw Puller*), released in 1955, and continued to work both in front of and behind the camera. In 1963, he received an award as Asia's Most Versatile Talent for his performance in *Ibu Mertuaku* (*My Mother-in-law*), a story of a successful and well-loved musician that mirrored his own life. When Ramlee died at age 44, he had amassed an impressive body of work; he had sung almost 360 songs, acted in 63 movies, and directed 34 feature films.[2] Even today, Ramlee is well loved. A 2008 theater production, *P. Ramlee, the Musical,* was a hit.

The local filmmaking industry declined in the 1960s for various reasons. Besides sociopolitical unrest that stunted industry growth, there was fierce competition from Hollywood films with their color technology. The introduction of television in 1963 further reduced the attractiveness of cinema-going. Entertainment was now more accessible to a wider audience at a lower cost and in the comfort of their own homes. The film studios eventually closed their Malaysian studios in the 1970s, and film production came to a standstill. Despite the lack of local films, cinema-viewing was popular with Singapore and Malaysian audiences, who subsisted on a diet of films mainly from Hollywood, Hong Kong, and India.

With the closing of the large film studios, independent filmmakers began to play a major role in local film production. In Singapore, the creation of an annual International Film Festival in 1987 and the launch of its short-film festival in 1991 were instrumental in identifying and supporting emerging local filmmakers. At the same time, the Malaysian and Singaporean governments played critical roles in supporting the industry. In Malaysia, the National Film Development Corporation Malaysia (or FINAS) was established in 1981 as a federal agency with powers to develop and regulate the industry. The creation of the agency and the incentives it administered helped restart film production, resulting in a bumper crop of local films in the 1980s. Notable filmmakers of this period include Othman Hafsham, who produced *Adik Manja* (*Lovable Baby*, 1980), *Mekanik* (*Mechanic*, 1983) and *Rahsia* (*The Secret*, 1986). He has since moved on to become a successful TV sitcom producer-director. The common themes of films of this period were nationalism, independence, and culture, reflecting the concerns of the period. Through the 1990s and up to the present day, the government has continued supporting the film industry and has even formulated a National Film Policy (NFP) to raise the standard of Malaysian films to international levels and to make Malaysia a regional centre of filmmaking.

In 1998, the Singapore government also began to more actively fund the film industry with the creation of the Singapore Film Commission. Besides funding feature films, the Commission provided funding for co-productions, short films, script development, and education. The focus on local filmmaking has been on current issues of Singapore life, specifically the challenges of urban life. Singapore's most successful filmmakers include Eric Khoo and Jack Neo. Khoo's art house film *12 Storeys* (1997) painted a bleak picture of everyday life in Singapore's ubiquitous public housing estates but won critical acclaim at several international film festivals. Khoo has since gone on to produce a number of films such as *Be with Me* (2005) and *My Magic* (2008), which were Singapore's official entries for the annual Academy Awards in the foreign language category for their respective years. Jack Neo is known as a filmmaker with a common touch. A former television comedian, he has made films such as *Money No Enough* (1998) and *I Not Stupid* (2002), which address the challenges of living in Singapore's competitive and materialistic society. Both were box office hits, and Neo is the most successful local director in terms of ticket sales.

Radio

Radio first came to the region in the 1930s via enthusiastic amateurs who formed societies such as the Malayan Wireless Society, in Kuala Lumpur. In the immediate postwar years, radio was used effectively to combat Communist propaganda and to win over the "hearts and minds" of the local people during the Emergency (1948–1960, see Chapter 1). By the 1960s, radio had spread throughout Singapore and Malaysia. Most broadcasts could be termed infotainment, that is, a combination of information and entertainment. Information related mainly to government policies and projects, news, and the weather, while entertainment took the form of popular music and storytelling.

Today, radio has become more focused on entertainment, especially in the urban areas. There are increasing numbers of private radio stations, and most stations follow the U.S. radio show format, but with an emphasis on both Asian and Western popular music. With the exception of niche "arts" stations, it is rare to hear traditional music on the radio airwaves. The largest radio network in Singapore is MediaCorp radio, which operates 13 local FM stations and broadcasts in four languages. Malaysia has a host of national and regional, public and private radio stations. While radio is concerned mainly with entertainment in Singapore and the Malaysian cities, it continues to be a critical medium for disseminating information to the more remote areas of Malaysia.

Television

Since its inception in Malaysia and Singapore in 1963, television has become a part of everyday life. From the beginning, television broadcasting was controlled by the government and used to support the national agenda. In Malaysia, the government operates two channels: TV1 (now RTM 1) and TV2 (now RTM2), which present a range of educational programs, news and entertainment in Malay, English, and the other languages spoken in Malaysia. Since 1985, licenses have been granted to private broadcasters such as TV3, as well as to cable and satellite television operators such as INTV, Mega TV, and Astro Television. In Singapore, television and radio services also first came under direct government control—Radio and Television Singapura (RTS), a unit of the Ministry of Culture until 1980. Between 1980 and the 1990s, radio and television services were under the auspices of the Singapore Broadcasting Corporation, a government statutory board, but have since been privatized. Since 2001, television and radio services have been provided by a private company, MediaCorp (Media Corporation of Singapore), which is still indirectly owned by the government.

Despite increasing privatization of the media in both countries, government censorship of broadcast media is still strong. In both countries, but especially in Malaysia, programs with high levels of sexual, violent, and political content are censored or disallowed, as they are seen to be incompatible with the more conservative values of local society. It is for this reason that there is strong political and social pressure to produce local television programs even though foreign programs are cheaper to purchase and often bring in more advertising revenue. In Malaysia especially, many Western productions do not meet Islamic values and mores. Even in Singapore, there is some ambivalence toward the Western values portrayed on the small screen. As the chairman of the Singapore Broadcasting Corporation, a predecessor of MediaCorp, once noted, "Western values and standards are being introduced all the time. We must therefore produce our own programs . . . suited to our society."[3]

Malaysia began producing local Malay dramas in the 1960s, and by the 1970s, RTM was producing dramas on a weekly basis. Television dramas were seen to play an important role in nation-building, and their themes often had moral, social, and political messages and encouraged the pursuit of development and harmony in a multiethnic society. The number of dramas increased as television became privatized in the 1980s and 1990s, which resulted in more time slots available for them. These newer dramas had fewer political goals and are centered around popular stories of crime, mystery, love, and family.

Singapore began to actively produce local television programs in the 1980s, with a focus on Chinese drama serials. Many of the producers, directors, and scriptwriters came from Hong Kong, the leader in the production of drama serials in Asia at the time. Landmark serials included *The Awakening* (1984), a million-dollar 26-episode historical drama that dealt with the lives of Singapore's early immigrants. Since the 1990s, local Chinese dramas become an established part of Singapore life, with nearly 1 million Singaporeans tuning into these dramas every night.[4] With a stronghold on the local market, MediaCorp has turned to producing dramas that are marketed regionally, and it now actively produces drama serials jointly with countries such as Malaysia and China. In addition, MediaCorp also produces English-language serials and has its greatest success with comedies such as *Under One Roof* and *Phua Chu Kang.* The latter was popular both in Singapore and in Malaysia for its lead character, an uncouth but funny building contractor who uses Singlish—the local form of English.

Cable and satellite television were introduced in the 1990s, and their appearance has had a significant impact on television audiences. Audiences now have a wider range of programs and films to watch, and it has become harder for the respective governments to control the kind of programs their citizens are watching. On a positive note, the competition from cable and satellite television has spurred local broadcasters to improve the quality and relevance of their programs.

NOTES

1. See Timothy White, "When Singapore Was Southeast Asia's Hollywood," *The Arts 5* (December 1997).

2. Raphael Millet, *Singapore Cinema* (Singapore: Editions Didier Millet, 2006), p. 48.

3. May Lin Loong, *On Television in Singapore* (Singapore: Singapore Broadcasting Corporation, 1988).

4. "New Directions," *Straits Times,* April 27, 1991.

SUGGESTED READINGS

Edi Sedyawati (ed.). *The Theatre of ASEAN.* Brunei Darussalam: ASEAN Committee on Culture and Information, 2001.

Ghulam-Sarwar Yousof (ed.). *The Encyclopedia of Malaysia, Vol. 8: Performing Arts.* Singapore: Archipelago Press, 1998.

Matusky, Patricia, and Tan Sooi Beng. *The Music of Malaysia: The Classical, Folk and Syncretic Traditions.* Aldershot: Ashgate, 2004.

McDaniel, Drew O. *Broadcasting in the Malay World: Radio, Television and Video in Brunei, Indonesia, Malaysia and Singapore.* Norwood, NJ: Ablex, 1994.

Millet, Raphael. *Singapore Cinema.* Singapore: Editions Didier Millet, 2006.

Santos, Ramon P. (ed.). *The Musics of ASEAN.* Brunei Darussalam: ASEAN Committee on Culture and Information, 1995.

Van der Heide, William. *Malaysian Cinema, Asian Film.* Amsterdam: Amsterdam University Press, 2002.

Zainal Abiddin Tinggal. (ed.). *The Dances of ASEAN.* Brunei Darussalam: ASEAN Committee on Culture and Information, 1998.

5

Housing and Architecture

HOUSING AND ARCHITECTURE in Singapore and Malaysia are a blend of old and new, traditional and modern, and a heady mix of European and Asian cultures. It is useful to think of the Singapore/Malaysia landscape as a palimpsest—a manuscript that has been written over many times, with some of the older writing still visible under the new ones. Singapore is a highly urbanized city of skyscrapers and modern buildings. Yet, sitting next to the gleaming glass and steel buildings are grand colonial buildings, quaint shophouses, and historical places of worship saved for posterity by active conservation policies. Across the causeway, the Malaysian state of Johor presents a vastly different landscape of small towns and houses among acres of rubber and oil palm plantations. Further along the western coastline, the historical town of Malacca is home to the oldest surviving buildings on the Peninsula. In the town square, the remnants of a 16th-century Portuguese fortress and 17th-century Dutch government offices have become tourist attractions. The narrow streets are lined with picturesque shophouses in the "eclectic Straits" style, an intriguing blend of East and West. Two hours away, the Malaysian capital, Kuala Lumpur, or KL, as it is more commonly known, boasts of Malaysia's most important icon of modernity—the 88-story Petronas Twin Towers—recognized as the tallest building in the world in 1996.

Tourism has affected the landscape and lifestyles in many coastal regions and offshore islands in Malaysia. In Pangkor Island, off the mainland's western coastline, islanders continue to live in rough timber stilt houses while wealthy tourists stay in the neighboring luxurious look-alikes at the six-star Pangkor Laut Resort (the late tenor Luciano Pavarotti once stayed there). In popular tourist destinations such as the islands of Langkawi and Tioman, large modern resorts and hotels as well as cafes, restaurants, bars, and shops have sprouted in recent years to cater to the growing tourist trade. The rural landscape dominates the northern states of Kedah and Kelantan. Here, the local villages or *kampung*s and a slower pace of life persist. In the East Malaysian states of Sabah and Sarawak, the respective capital cities of Kota Kinabalu and Kuching are rapidly modernizing. However, along the rivers and waterways one can still see the traditional indigenous houses that are still home to the many indigenous tribes.

TRADITIONAL HOUSING

Prior to the arrival of the European colonialists, traditional housing in the Peninsula consisted of simple structures whose basic designs were determined by their functions and the availability of materials. Many of these structures have since either given way to more modern ones or have been given a facelift through the use of modern construction methods and materials.

Forest Dwellings

On the mainland, the Orang Asli used to, and continue to, live mainly in the forests. Being originally nomadic, the Orang Asli built houses that provided only the basics and that were made from available resources: young hardwood for standing poles, bamboo for the walls, and woven leaves of wild palms for thatched roofs. Huts raised high above the ground usually have large windows, while those closer to the ground have only narrow slits or no windows at all. There is traditionally only one door, made of bark or sackcloth, to the house. Bathhouses are often communal and lavatory facilities nonexistent, making a toilet stop literally a response to the "call of nature."

The Longhouse

The longhouse is the traditional form of dwelling among the indigenous tribes of Sabah and Sarawak. In Sarawak, most longhouse settlements are built along the open banks of rivers and streams, which are ready sources of water and fish, as well as the major means of transportation. In general, the longhouse is made of timber and raised on wooden stilts at least 20 feet above the ground. Although designs vary among the tribes, all longhouses are communal, with private areas for individual families and shared areas for the longhouse community. A longhouse usually has 20 to 80 small family units placed side by side and linked by a long common corridor, giving the structure its name. Besides individual units owned by a family, there are communal spaces such as the gallery where social activities take place, and the open deck where crops and laundry are dried. A longhouse can usually accommodate between 200 and 300 people and are still used by the Iban, Melanau, Orang Ulu, and Bidayuh in Sarawak, and the Murut, Bajau, Lotud, and Bonggi people in Sabah.

In recent years, as indigenous groups have been encouraged to adopt more sedentary lifestyles, the longhouses have also begun to take on a more permanent form. The use of materials such as galvanized iron, concrete, and glass is becoming more common. The only objections to the use of these modern materials have come from the tourist industry, for which longhouse tourism is a booming business. Tour operators have been known to advise longhouse communities to make alterations to their longhouse structures to make them appear more authentic and traditional in order to appeal to tourists.[1]

Kampungs and the Traditional Malay House

The Malays, who also believe in strong communal ties, traditionally live in *kampungs* (villages). The *kampung* typically comprises several Malay houses whose boundaries are demarcated by clusters of trees at the corners. Having no physical barriers such as fences between houses, the *kampung* has an open and informal atmosphere that promotes communal activities. Lacking individual

Traditional *kampung* houses built of timber can still be seen around villages and towns all over Malaysia. Courtesy of the author.

utilities, villagers used to gather at wells and rivers to collect water, bathe, and do their washing. The values of sharing and cooperation are emphasized in *kampung* life and are embedded in the idea of *gotong-royong* (sharing work with others).

Within the *kampung*, each family resides in its own home, commonly known as the Malay house. Although styles vary, the basic form and method of construction do not. Like the dwellings of the indigenous communities, Malay houses are constructed with local materials and are ideally suited for their environment. The traditional Malay house is mainly a timber structure built off the ground using the post and beam method. There are several basic elements to the Malay house that underlie all Malay architecture, albeit on a grander scale for *istanas* (palaces) and mosques. They include these principles:

1. The house is raised off the ground. This provides protection from floods, insects, and wild animals and allows the house to be ventilated through cracks in the raised floor.

2. It has an open layout. The house is divided into areas rather than rooms, with a noticeable absence of partitions and walls. This reflects the emphasis on strong family bonds over individual privacy in Malay culture.

3. It has steeply pitched roofs to allow rainwater to drain off rapidly and warm air to rise to increase ventilation. The roof is also covered with *atap* made from the fronds of the *nipah, rumbia,* or *bertam* palm, which holds little heat in the day and cools down at night. The beauty of the Malay house is that its entire design is aimed at ensuring a continuous flow of air through the house and out of the roof so that the interior remains cool and comfortable despite the humid tropical heat.

4. It is modular in concept. Construction begins with the main house or *rumah ibu* (mother house), which is used for sleeping and for entertaining important guests during festivals. As the needs or resources of the family increase, additions such as the *rumah dapur* (kitchen), *serambi* (veranda), and *anjung* (entrance porch) can be attached to the main house.

While many *kampung*s have disappeared through urbanization, a number still survive, albeit in a modified form. More durable materials and modern sanitation and conveniences have been introduced to make these traditional houses more compatible with modern life. The satellite dish has also become a feature of these traditional houses as more and more Malaysians, whether living in the cities or villages, gain access to satellite television.

EUROPEAN ARCHITECTURE

The Europeans have been a strong cultural force in Singapore and Malaysia since the 16th century, and their architectural legacy can still be clearly seen in the region. In Malacca, the architectural influences of the Portuguese and the Dutch are still strong. The most significant Portuguese structure is the A Famosa fort, built soon after the Portuguese captured Malacca in 1511. Its formidable walls, which reputably took more than 36 years to complete, were the main source of protection of the Portuguese town built within it. It withstood attacks for 130 years until it was eventually destroyed by the Dutch in 1670, but some remnants of the fort still exist. The most prominent buildings reflecting Dutch influence are the Stadthuys (town hall), which was the residence of the Dutch governor and also held government offices, and Christ Church, completed in 1753. These buildings have been preserved as examples of Dutch architecture, masonry, and woodworking of the 17th century. Although both buildings were originally white, they have since been painted red.

British influence is still strongly felt in Singapore, historically the most important British colony in this region. To facilitate the governance and growth of the island and its territories in the Peninsula, the British constructed numerous government and commercial buildings, many of which still stand today. These public government buildings were typically brick and mortar buildings in either the Palladian/neoclassical or Gothic style, depending on what was vogue in Britain at the time. The Palladian and neoclassical styles are characterized by the use of the architectural style of ancient Greece and Rome. This includes the use of columns, decorative motifs, and simple geometric compositions. These buildings were concentrated in the central business district south of the island. A number of these buildings have survived but have since been rebuilt and refurbished to serve new functions. The oldest surviving government building in Singapore is the Old Parliament House, designed along neoclassical lines. It was originally built as a private house for the merchant John Maxwell in 1826 and was later acquired by the government. At one point it served as a courthouse; later, it housed the Legislative Assembly. From 1965 to 1999, the building served as Parliament House for Singapore's government. Since 2000, the building has once again been refurbished, and it is now an arts venue and gallery known as The Arts House.

Kuala Lumpur's architecture was also dramatically affected by the British, especially after the city became the capital of the Federated Malay States (FMS) in 1896. The buildings constructed by the British in KL were, however, different from those in Singapore. Instead of strictly following Western architectural traditions, the British sought to incorporate Asian features. One such example is the Sultan Abdul Samad building, completed in 1896 to house the colonial government's secretariat. A neoclassical style was initially proposed, but the state engineer, C. E. Spooner, rejected this design. Spooner advocated the use of a style more in tune with the Islamic culture of the area. The building was subsequently resigned in a Moorish style with onion-shaped domes and pointed horseshoe arches. The building did include some Western elements such as classical pediments and a symmetrical façade. This mixture of Asian elements and classical, Gothic, and Renaissance components resulted in a unique style, sometimes referred to as the British Raj style. Other government buildings built along these lines include the General Post Office, the Municipality Building, and the FMS Survey Department Building.

The influx of European expatriates in the second half of the 19th century also brought about a need for buildings and spaces where the expatriate population could worship, play, and live. In terms of recreation, the British used similar designs in Singapore and Kuala Lumpur. In both towns, recreation revolved around "The Padang," a flat, grassy plain that could be used for cricket, lawn tennis, parades, and official occasions. Surrounding the Padang were the clubhouses of expatriate recreational clubs—the Singapore Cricket Club in Singapore and the Selangor Club in Kuala Lumpur. On the edge of Singapore's Padang are the Victoria Memorial Hall and the Victoria Theatre, which have, since the early 20th century, served as venues for dramatic and musical entertainments.

The typical British expatriate home was the bungalow—a stand-alone house in neoclassical style adjusted to suit the Southeast Asian environment and climate. The homes were designed on the principles of the traditional Malay house to ensure that the house was well ventilated and cool, but they were built using Western materials such as brick, tile, and stucco to make them more durable and fire-resistant than their Malay counterparts. In addition, classical elements such as Roman columns and ornamentation were added to the frontage to enhance the prestige of the house. This style has become known as the "Anglo-Straits" architectural style and has been attributed to G. D. Coleman. Coleman was one of the most influential architects at that time, having designed a number of churches and buildings in Singapore, including the Armenian Church, which still stands today.

CHINESE ARCHITECTURE

One of the architectural styles unique to Singapore and Malaysia is the "Straits Chinese" style, attributed to the Peranakans. Just like their language and culture, the architectural design of their homes is a curious fusion of Chinese, Malay, and Western elements. The Peranakan house is a narrow but deep townhouse. One of its distinctive features is a pair of half-doors, known as *pintu pagar* or fence door, in front of the main doors. While similar to the swinging doors typically seen at bars in America's old West, these half-doors are usually intricately carved and painted in gold. They provide the household with some privacy when the main doors are left open in the day, while at the same time letting in light and ventilation. As the Peranakans were usually well-to-do, the façades of their houses are ornately and colorfully decorated with glazed tiles, carved decoration, and floral plasterwork. The interior of the houses are made up of public and private areas connected by covered passages and interior courtyards. The courtyards or air wells allow light into what would otherwise be dark and dank houses. The rooms have high ceilings and are furnished with commissioned blackwood furniture inlaid with marble and mother of pearl. Some of these Peranakan houses can still be found in Singapore and Malacca. While some remain private residences, many have been converted to boutique hotels and offices. Some of the most authentic re-creations of traditional Peranakan houses today are the Baba and Nonya Museum in Malacca's Heeren Street and the Baba House Museum in Singapore.

Another unique architectural form in Singapore and Malaysia is the shophouse. The shophouse was commonly found in urban centers where the Chinese congregated. Most of these building are only two or three stories high. The ground floor was typically used for business and served as the shop front, while the family usually resided on the second floor. In most cases, the second floor was subdivided into numerous rooms that housed several

The Peranakan house is a narrow but deep townhouse, usually with an ornate façade. Many of these houses, such as this one in Malacca, have been converted into museums, offices, boutique hotels, or clan associations. Courtesy of the author.

families. Made of brick, plaster, concrete, and timber, the shophouses built in the 19th century were around 20 feet wide and 100 feet deep. Each unit was connected to the others to form a block and shared a continuous, covered walkway. The five-foot way was so called because in 1822, the British administration specified that all shophouses had to include a veranda at least 5 feet wide on the ground floor. The original purpose was to create pedestrian linkages that would shade and protect the retail outlets. The five-foot way has since become a distinctive feature of shophouses in the region. Beyond the basic features described, shophouse façades and external designs varied according to the fashionable styles of the time. There are shophouses whose façades incorporate elements of Neoclassical, Dutch Patrician, and Art Deco styles. Shophouses can still be found in Singapore's Chinatown and in the commercial center of almost every Malaysian town. While some families still live above the shops, many of these shophouses have been converted to boutique shops and office spaces.

PLACES OF WORSHIP

Mosques

Mosques and *suraus* (prayer halls) sprang up around the Peninsula as Islam's influence spread. These places of worship share certain design features. At the entrance, there is usually a covered porch where footwear can be deposited. After removing their footwear, worshippers proceed to an ablution area for ritual cleansing before they enter the prayer hall, which faces Mecca, the holy city of Islam. A tall, slender tower known as a minaret is a central feature of most mosques. It is used to call Muslims to prayer and to indicate the location of the mosque, which is especially important in urban areas. The first mosques were probably timber buildings in the style of wooden Hindu temples in Southeast Asia. However, because of the fragility of these materials, none of these older mosques have survived. The oldest surviving mosque in this style is the 18th-century Kampung Laut Mosque in Kelantan.

The British built a number of mosques in Malaysia in the 19th century for the Malay rulers and revealed British architects' unfamiliarity with mosque design. On one hand, there were mosques based almost entirely on the classical Western architecture tradition such as Kuala Lumpur's Jamek Mosque (completed in 1925), which has Gothic towers, Doric columns, and French windows. On the other hand, there were mosques such as the Ubudiah Mosque, also in Kuala Lumpur, whose design was based on the Moorish tradition, with Moghul-style onion-shaped domes, horizontal banding, and octagonal minarets. There was thus considerable variation in design as architects experimented with different design traditions. However, as these

The minaret of a mosque is a key architectural feature. Courtesy of the author.

mosques were built with a mixture of concrete, brick, and plaster, they out-lived and overshadowed their timber counterparts.

Since Malaysia's independence, mosque design has been influenced by Western modernism, with the Masjid Negara (the National Mosque) starting the trend. This mosque, built in 1965 in Kuala Lumpur and constructed of reinforced concrete with Italian marble finishing, reflects a mixture of Islamic and modernist design principles. Its interiors were designed according to the principles of "form follows functions," while its unusual umbrella-shaped roof represents a synthesis of the Middle Eastern dome tradition and the pyramidal forms of indigenous architecture. Other mosques built along these lines include the Taman Tun Mosque and the Sarawak State Mosque, both completed in 1990.

In Singapore, while historical mosques, such as the Sultan Mosque and the Hajjah Fatimah Mosque, continue to be part of the Muslim community's religious life, they also attract a large number of non-Muslim tourists and visitors. In the 1970s, with rapid urban development, the government and the Muslim community have worked together to construct mosques in every housing estate. In addition to retaining their religious functions, these new-generation mosques are also equipped with conference rooms, classrooms, halls, and even auditoriums to accommodate a wide range of activities for the Muslim communities. Often, they are regarded as Islamic community centers for education and social activities as well.

Churches

The European colonization of the region saw the arrival of missionaries and priest-architects who actively built schools and churches as part of their evangelical efforts and to cater to the religious needs of the expatriate community. The Portuguese built churches as part of their mission to spread the Roman Catholic faith. St Paul's Church in Malacca survives today as the oldest Catholic church in Malaysia. Christ Church, built by the Dutch in the 18th century, is the oldest Protestant church in Southeast Asia. Penang claims to be the site of the earliest Anglican church service in the region, held in the classical-style St. George the Martyr Church, completed in 1818. The oldest church in Singapore is the Armenian Church, built in 1821 and designed by G. D. Coleman in the classical style. This was followed by other churches, such as the Convent of the Holy Infant Jesus, which consisted of a girls' school and a chapel, in 1854, and the St. Andrew's Cathedral in the mid-19th century. The latter was designed following the Early English style of the 12th century. It was from this cathedral that the Anglican evangelical outreach in Singapore was launched.

Chinese Temples

Among the first buildings the Chinese migrants constructed were temples. These were built according to the architectural traditions of southern China, from which most of the migrants came. The temples were initially humble structures, but, as the wealth of the community grew, the temples became grander and more elaborate. Despite variations in scale and grandeur, the temples followed a layout that remained formal and symmetrical. The temple consists of a series of halls opening into courtyards along a vertical axis. While the number of halls varies, there is usually a prayer pavilion where worshippers offer initial prayers. There is also usually a main hall where the shrine of the resident deity is placed and where incense and food offerings may be placed. The design and structure of the Chinese temple is highly symbolic of the Chinese belief system. The roof ridge is often decorated with auspicious animals such as dragons, phoenixes, and fish, along with pearls and pagodas. The color red is also used extensively as it represents the sun and suggests prosperity and festivity. As symbolism, mythology and geomancy (or *feng shui*) shape the architecture of the Chinese temples, and their design has remained consistent over time.

The roof ridges of many Chinese temples are decorated extensively with auspicious animals such as dragons, phoenixes, and fish. Courtesy of the author.

The oldest temple in Malaysia, and reputably Southeast Asia, is the Cheng Hoon Teng Temple, or Temple of the Evergreen Clouds, in Malacca. Said to be founded in 1641 by the leader of the Chinese community, Lee Wei King, the actual building was completed only in 1704. Like many typical Chinese temples in the region, it features dragons on its roof ridges and images of birds, plants, and bamboo, all considered auspicious by the Chinese. Singapore's oldest Chinese temple is the Thian Hock Keng (Temple of Heavenly Bliss). It was first built as a simple joss house in 1821 before being rebuilt as a temple in 1839. Dedicated to Ma Zhu Po (Goddess of the Sea), the Thian Hock Keng was the first place of call for new Chinese immigrants, who came to the temple to give thanks for their safe passage to the island. As at many other temples, the entrance to the temple is decorated with figures from Chinese mythology who guard the temple. The image of Ma Zhu Po is placed in the main hall together with Guan Gong (God of war) and Bao Sheng Da Di (Protector of Life). Within the temple walls are also areas that house ancestor tablets where the spirits of ancestors are said to reside. Family members visit the tablets and make offerings to their ancestors here.

Indian Temples

Although one of the smallest ethnic communities in Singapore and Malaysia, the Indians have made their presence felt through the building of Hindu temples. While simple shrines and temples have existed in the region for several centuries, it was only with the influx of Indian migrants during the 19th century that temples were built in larger and grander proportions and in far greater numbers. The Indian community is a diverse group comprising different subgroups, and temple designs vary accordingly. The most striking temples are those built by the South Indians, who make up the majority of the Indian population in Singapore and Malaysia.

To Hindus, the temple is not only a place of worship; it is also "where the gods make themselves visible."[2] The sacred images and symbols of the deity to whom the temple is dedicated are housed in the temple's innermost sanctum, known as the *garbagraham*. The *garbagraham* is the essence of the temple. The temple's interior spaces are arranged to encourage the movement of devotees from the outside toward the sanctuary through a series of spaces that become increasingly sacred. In most temples, devotees prostrate themselves before the *kodisthampam* (flagpole) in the first area. Next, they move on to the *palidbeedam* (sacrificial altar), where priests place food offerings and flowers. It is here that devotees pray on their knees. The *vaganam* (vehicle for the deity) resides in the third area, and devotees wait here as the priests enter the *garbagraham* (sanctum) to bring offerings to the image

The most eye-catching feature of the South Indian temple is its entrance tower, the *gopuram*. It usually consists of at least five tiers of figures representing the various incarnations of Lord Shiva and other legendary characters. Courtesy of the author.

of the deity on their behalf. The most eye-catching feature of the South Indian temple is its entrance tower, known as the *gopuram*. This consists of five or more tiers of figures, each figure representing one of the various incarnations of Lord Shiva and other legendary characters. The *gopuram* of the Sri Srinvasa Perumal Temple in Singapore is 60 feet high and has six tiers of sculptures. The main door of the temple may be carved out of teak or sandalwood to depict scenes from legends, and statues may stand guard on either side of the door. Within the temple are often highly decorated ceilings and columns that not only depict the gods but retell their stories in vibrant colors.

INDEPENDENCE AND BEYOND

When Singapore and Malaysia became independent nations, both embarked on policies to promote economic growth through industrialization and modernization. These policies brought about dramatic changes in the homes people lived in.

Modern Housing

In Singapore, more than 80 percent of the population now live in high-rise flats built by the government. This is unlike the pre-independence era of the 1950s and 1960s, when most people lived in overcrowded shophouses, in dilapidated squatters, or in rural *kampungs*. The Housing and Development Board (HDB) was formed in 1960 to address the housing crisis, and it embarked on an ambitious plan to build high-rise and high-density flats to house the island's growing population. The earliest flats were very small, with only one or two separate bedrooms. They were, however, clean and fire-resistant and came with built-in amenities such as running water, electricity, and toilets, which traditional houses lacked. These flats were sold to residents at subsidized rates, and, with the help of a government-supported home ownership scheme, almost 80 percent of residents now own their homes. By the year 2000, HDB had built more than 800,000 homes.

With the housing crisis eased and Singaporeans becoming more affluent, the design and layout of HDB flats improved to cater to rising expectations. Newer HDB flats were larger, with four-room (consisting of three bedrooms and a living room) and five-room flats (three bedrooms, a living room, and a dining room) becoming the norm. Greater planning also went into the design of housing estates to ensure that they had adequate infrastructure and amenities such as shops, markets, food centers (buildings where food stalls are congregated), schools, and community services and that they were linked to the city and other areas through an efficient bus and rail system. One of

Singapore's largest housing estates, Tampines New Town, with a population of around 230,000, won the prestigious World Habitat Award in 1993. This award was given as recognition of an outstanding contribution to human settlement and development. With a slowdown in new housing projects, the focus of the HDB is to upgrade and improve the flats. Since the early 1990s, the government has worked with private developers to improve the quality and design of the flats. One of the latest government housing projects is the Pinnacle@ Duxton, which is expected to be completed in 2010. This project includes the construction of 50-story apartment blocks with features such as sky bridges, a jogging track, a sky garden, and commercial and social facilities.

In Malaysia, the most common form of modern housing is the linear linkhouse or terrace house. Initiated either as private developments or jointly with state governments, these housing estates are often developed with the provision that a percentage of built units be low-cost with controlled prices. As Malaysia is a far larger country than Singapore and has fewer pressures on land use, low-rise houses are more practical and economical to build than are high-rise apartments. The typical linkhouse occupies a rectangular lot of land area between 420 and 550 square feet with house lots arranged linearly back-to-back. As in Singapore, these housing projects are clustered in estates

The majority of Singaporeans live in high-rise apartments found all over the island. Most of these apartments are built by the Housing and Development Board and are hence known as HDB flats. Courtesy of the author.

with basic infrastructure such as schools, mosques, playgrounds, and shops. However, as many of these are private developments with little governmental control, the houses often suffer from poor workmanship and design. Some of the largest housing estates are in the Klang Valley on the outskirts of Kuala Lumpur.

With growing affluence in recent years, private condominiums have become popular in Malaysia and Singapore. In a sense, the condominium is a marriage between the high-rise apartment and the country club. Condominiums are usually in exclusive or choice locations, are nicely landscaped, come with security surveillance, and have recreational facilities such as swimming pools, tennis courts, and even golf putting greens. High-rise condominiums often offer the added advantage of panoramic views, although this is less relevant in Singapore, which is densely populated and filled with high-rise buildings. In both countries, the ownership of a condominium has become a status symbol.

Cityscapes and National Icons

Singapore, in a matter of four decades, has become a wholly urban city. Since the 1960s, Singapore has embarked on major urban renewal in its city center that has included the demolition of many older structures in favor of newer, taller, and more modern buildings. In land-scarce Singapore, there is a strong need to optimize the use of land, and thus buildings were constructed skyward and designed for multiple purposes. Singapore's first skyscraper was the modest 18-story Asia Insurance Building, built in 1954. This was followed by numerous commercial buildings, each built taller than its predecessors. Some of the distinctive landmarks in the Singapore city skyline include the OCBC Building, which resembles a huge calculator, an appropriate motif for a bank. It was designed by international architect I. M. Pei and was built in 1975. Other distinctive buildings include the steel, glass, and aluminum Hitachi Tower, built in 1993, and UOB Plaza, designed by the Japanese architect Kenzo Tange and completed in 1995.

Given the pressures on land in Singapore, there is a strong focus on mixed-use developments. One of the earliest developments of this kind was the People's Park Complex in Chinatown, designed by a local architectural firm, Design Partnership (now known as DP Architects). This complex was the first shopping center in Southeast Asia to incorporate shops, offices, and homes under one roof. The led the way to more ambitious developments such as Raffles City, completed in 1985, which is described as a "city within a city." Raffles City occupies a complete city block and contains three hotels, a major shopping complex, and an office block. The even larger Suntec City development, launched in the mid-1990s, houses Singapore's largest mall, its largest convention center, and several office blocks surrounding the world's largest fountain, the Fountain of Wealth. Interestingly, despite the modern principles guiding its construction, Suntec City is also designed according to *feng shui* principles. *Feng shui* is the traditional Chinese art of geomancy, where buildings, interiors, and the landscape are ordered to capitalize on auspicious energy lines known as *qi*. In the case of Suntec City, the five office buildings are built like the five fingers of a hand, with the Fountain of Wealth right in the middle of the palm. This design was to generate prosperity and happiness for the complex's residents. The success of the development has been attributed to its prime *feng shui* configuration.

The skyscrapers and large retail and commercial developments all reflect Singapore's progress as a modern, developed nation. There has, however, been some criticism that most major projects have been commissioned to foreign architects who design in the International style common to modern cities across the world. This trend is seen to have hampered the development of a distinctive Singaporean architectural style, which is still in its nascent stages. In addition to finding its own distinctive architectural style, Singapore is also in the process of creating buildings that will serve as national icons. In the late 1960s, public buildings such as the National Theatre, the National Stadium and the National Library were constructed for this purpose. The National Theatre, opened in 1963, was jointly funded by the government and the public through "a dollar a brick" campaign and was the first national theater in the country. In the 1980s, it was found that the building was structurally unsound, and this led to its eventual demolition.

The latest venue for artistic and dramatic events is a contender for status as a national icon. Called "The Esplanade—Theatres on the Bay," the theater, with its distinctive spiky sunshades, is affectionately known to the locals as the "durian"—a local fruit with a green spiky skin and a pungent fragrance. This moniker did not sit well with the architects, who argue that the sunshades represent woven rattan walls in traditional Asian buildings. The National Stadium, opened in 1973, has been the venue for the nation's largest sporting, entertainment, and national events, including soccer matches and National Day parades. It has been scheduled for demolition to make way for a new 86.5-acre facility, the Singapore Sports Hub. The Hub will comprise a new 55,000-capacity National Stadium with a retractable roof, an indoor aquatic center with a seating capacity of 6,000, a 400-meter warm-up athletic track, and a 3,000-seater multipurpose arena, as well as commercial developments.

In Malaysia, the most dramatic changes are most visible in its capital, Kuala Lumpur. Even as the KL skyline became increasingly crowded with high-rise buildings constructed mostly in the bland International style, architects were also in the process of developing a distinctive Malaysian architectural style.

While this style continues to develop and change, its emergence was motivated by independence and by the need to create public buildings to serve as national symbols. Known as "neotraditionalism," this movement incorporated traditional Malay architectural elements into buildings with functional and modernist sensibilities. The most notable feature of this movement is the design of the roofs and silhouettes of the buildings, which echo the style of traditional houses. Examples of buildings in this style include the Muzium Negara (National Museum), whose doubled-pitched gabled roof resembles traditional roof forms, and Parliament House, whose concertina roof is supposed to resemble the Bugis roof form, and where the paneling on the 18-story tower block is supposed to resemble pineapple skin.

While the Malaysian government has been active in creating national architectural icons since independence, its latest structures project an image of Malaysia not only as a distinctive sovereign nation but as one that is dynamic and rapidly modernizing. Two of its most impressive architectural icons are the Petronas Twin Towers and the Kuala Lumpur International Airport (KLIA). The Petronas Twin Towers, standing 88 stories and 1,483 feet tall, are the most striking features of the Kuala Lumpur City Centre (KLCC). The complex, opened in the 1990s, encompasses a huge development that

The KL Petronas Twin Towers are the most eye-catching architectural feature of Malaysia's capital city, Kuala Lumpur. Courtesy of the author.

includes a concert hall, an art gallery, a mega shopping mall, a 13-screen cineplex, several office blocks, and a hotel, all on the fringe of a 50-acre public park. While the Petronas Twin Towers represent the epitome of modernity and are on the cutting edge of construction design and technology, they also represent the Malaysian identity. This is evident in the use of geometrical form, important in Islamic architecture, and in the use of Malaysian motifs such as *songket* weaving patterns in the building's interiors.

The KLIA was opened in 1998 to much fanfare as one of the most advanced airports in Asia. Its design by Japanese architect Kisho Kurokawa incorporates Malaysian characteristics within a functionalist approach. It presents a strong first statement on the growth and future of the nation to new arrivals who fly into this modern airport. The bustling city of Kuala Lumpur is also home to other "mega" projects such as Putrajaya and Cyberjaya. Putrajaya, the new federal political and administrative center, is planned and designed as a garden city to support a population of 500,000. Cyberjaya, with ambitions of becoming Malaysia's own Silicon Valley, will become an information technology hub and home to the Multimedia University. These projects are reflections of Malaysia's vision to become a developed nation by the year 2020.

NOTES

1. See Sallie Yea, "On and Off the Ethnic Tourism Map in Southeast Asia: The Case of Iban Longhouse Tourism, Sarawak, Malaysia," *Tourism Geographies* 4 (2), (May 2002): pp. 173–194.

2. George Michell, *The Hindu Temple: An Introduction to Its Meaning and Forms* (London: Paul Elek, 1977), p. 61.

SUGGESTED READINGS

Chen, Voon Fee (ed.). *The Encyclopedia of Malaysia, Vol. 5: Architecture.* Singapore: Archipelago Press, 1998.

Powell, Robert. *Singapore Architecture.* Hong Kong: Periplus Editions, 2004.

Yeang, Ken. *The Architecture of Malaysia.* Kuala Lumpur: Pepin Press, 1992.

6

Food and Fashion

THIS CHAPTER EXPLORES food and fashion in Singapore and Malaysia where tradition and modernity exist side by side, each inspiring and influencing the other. The first part of this chapter describes the culinary culture of the region and the distinctive features of Singapore and Malaysia food. Locals enjoy eating traditional food in hawker stalls and local coffee shops (known as *kopitiams*) even as they relish sampling new cuisines from different parts of the world in fast-food chains, cafés, and restaurants. As a meeting point of different cultures, much of the local cuisine, especially that of the Peranakans and Eurasians, is an intriguing blend of various food traditions. In Peranakan cuisine, for example, one can taste a blend of Malay spices and curries with Chinese sauces and ingredients. Eurasian food, on the other hand, is a synthesis of Western-style cooking of Portuguese, English, or Dutch origin, and local spices and ingredients.

The fashion of the region—traditional costumes and modern adaptations—is discussed in the second part of this chapter. Because Malaysia and Singapore have warm weather throughout the year, everyday fashion styles tend to be practical, favoring light casual wear. For festive occasions and formal functions, locals wear more elaborate clothes; each ethnic community has its own ethnic costumes. In addition, both the Singapore and the Malaysian governments have promoted national dress to build a sense of national identity and belonging, although with different degrees of success. With modernity and globalization, international clothing brands have become a mainstay of these two countries, and Singaporeans and Malaysians also follow international fashion trends.

Food Traditions

It is no exaggeration to say that Singaporeans and Malaysians are obsessed with food. In everyday life, conversations often center on food, with locals discussing what to eat for dinner right after lunch. There are also numerous local television shows and books devoted to food, ranging from instructional cooking shows to books or programs that recommend the best food outlets in the two countries. The ethnic food traditions range from simple and basic food eaten by the indigenous people to the sometimes complex and highly esteemed cuisines of the Chinese. Although ethnic cuisines have, over time, incorporated elements of other groups, they are still distinctive and are often deliberately kept separate because of the different dietary habits of the communities. The region has six main cuisine types: Indigenous, Malay, Chinese, Indian, Peranakan, and Eurasian. There are, however, unifying themes in the use of local spices and chilies.

Some local favorites: (from top left, clockwise) *ice kachang,* a sweet and cold dessert of syrupy ground ice, red beans, and jelly strips; *satay,* meat skewers grilled over a charcoal fire and dipped in a peanut sauce; *yong tau foo,* assorted items of various types of bean curd, fishballs, and vegetables in clear soup; and chicken rice balls. Courtesy of the author.

Indigenous

The food of the indigenous people has traditionally been simple. Ingredients are taken from the immediate natural environment and prepared using basic cooking methods. One of the dishes distinctive of Sarawak's ethnic groups is *umai,* a raw fish salad in which bite-sized slivers of fish are marinated with lime juice, salt, sliced onions, ginger, and chili. A traditional lunch of the Melanau fishermen, *umai* is usually eaten with a bowl of toasted sago pearls, found abundantly in Sarawak. Sabah also has a version of the *umai* known as *hinava,* which is prepared with a slight variation in ingredients.

Sago-based dishes are common among the tribes of Sabah and Sarawak. Sago is used as the main starch component in the local dishes, as the swampy environment makes it unsuitable for rice cultivation. One such dish is *linut,* a thick sago paste usually eaten with *sambal* (chili with shrimp paste). This dish is known as *ambuyat* in Sabah. Another Melanau delicacy is the *siat,* sago grubs stir-fried with ginger and shallots. These grubs are considered a good source of protein. Rice wine is as common a drink in Sabah and Sarawak as beer is in Western countries. Sarawak's traditional drink is known as *tuak,* a potent brew made from fermented rice, yeast, and sugar. This drink is served at almost every major ceremony and is also popular for everyday consumption. In Sabah, the rice wine is known as *tapai* or *pengasai* and is often featured in traditional ceremonies and ritual offerings.

Unlike the food of the other ethnic groups, indigenous cuisine is not popular among the other ethnic groups, so there are few opportunities to taste this kind of food. The best opportunity to sample this type of cuisine is during a visit to these communities or at a cultural tourism site in East Malaysia.

Malay

As Muslims, Malays have to conform to strict dietary rules. All the food they consume must be *halal*—in conformance with Muslim laws. According to these laws, consumption of pork in its various forms, such as bacon, ham, and lard, is forbidden, as the pig is considered an "unclean" animal. Furthermore, the handling and preparation of other types of meat, including the way the livestock is reared and killed, has to be in accordance with strict regulations. Although the use of utensils are not proscribed by Muslim laws, Malays traditionally eat with their fingers rather than with forks and spoons. Malays also take care only to eat with their right hand, as the left hand is used for cleaning purposes. The cleanliness of the hands is very important, and at a formal dinner, such as a wedding, it is common for waiters to go around with pots of water for guests to clean their hands before and after the meal.

Malay food is typically hot and spicy. The identifying characteristics of Malay cuisine include the liberal use of spices, coconut milk, and rice as a meal staple. Fragrant roots such as galangal, ginger and fresh turmeric; aromatics such as shallots, garlic, fresh and dried chilies, lemongrass, and *belachan* (dried shrimp paste) are also common ingredients in Malay dishes. There is, however, some regional variation. Because of their proximity to Thailand, the northern Malaysian states are influenced by Thai cuisine and prefer their dishes sour and spicy with heavy use of tamarind pulp and chili. The states on the west coast are more influenced by Indonesia and prefer milder curries cooked with coconut milk.

A popular Malay dish is *nasi lemak* (literally translated as coconut rice), which is usually eaten for breakfast or lunch. A scoop of fragrant rice cooked in coconut milk is served with an assortment of condiments such as *sambal* chili, cucumber slices, deep fried *ikan bilis* (anchovies), and a hard-boiled egg. More elaborate versions may include substantial meat dishes such as *satay*, spicy meat skewers barbequed over hot charcoal and served with a peanut sauce, and *beef rendang*, beef curry slow-cooked with spices and coconut. Malay meals at home typically consist of white rice with a range of cooked food such as curries, fish, vegetables, and chicken. Noodle dishes such as *mee siam*, thin rice vermicelli in a hot and spicy sauce, and *mee rebus*, yellow noodles in a thick curry sauce, are also popular.

Although there is a substantial range of traditional dishes, new dishes are constantly being invented. A relatively newer Malay dish is the *roti john*, created by a street hawker in the 1970s initially for his Caucasian and Eurasian clientele. The dish marries the European egg and toast breakfast with local spicy meats, onions, and tomato sauce. Its name, *roti john*, was coined by combining the Malay term for bread—"roti"—with "John," a name used by locals to refer to any European.

Chinese

The Chinese in Singapore and Malaysia come from different regions and dialect groups, each with its own food traditions. The Cantonese are known for their soups and roasted meat products, the Teochews for their braised poultry in soy sauce, and the Hainanese for chicken rice and local-style Western dishes. Regardless of their dialect allegiance, the Chinese often eat cuisine associated with people who speak different dialects or even different ethnic groups. With few religious dietary limitations, the Chinese are often the most adventurous eaters.

Like those of the Malays, the typical Chinese meals prepared at home consist of white rice eaten with a variety of cooked dishes such as a soup and stir-fried dishes that include seafood, vegetables, and meat. Although traditionally the Chinese eat with chopsticks, it is now common for them to use a spoon and a fork when eating rice-based meals. The Chinese also often eat out, traditionally at hawker stalls, hawker centers, or at the coffee shop (*kopitiam*). Popular Chinese dishes for lunch and dinner include *kon lo mee* (noodles with soy sauce and roasted pork), *char kway teow* (fried flat noodles in dark sauce), *chai tow kway* (fried radish cake with eggs), and *bak chor mee* (egg noodles with minced meat and vinegar). Seafood is also a perennial favorite, with one of Singapore's signature dishes being chili crab—large fresh mud crabs served with a fiery tomato chili sauce. The Chinese also often eat elaborate banquets at restaurants to celebrate occasions such as weddings and birthdays. The typical Chinese banquet consists of at least eight dishes, usually including delicacies such as shark's fin, abalone, and sea cucumber.

Although different varieties of Chinese cuisine are available in Singapore and Malaysia, many dishes have been localized to suit local tastes. Because of their exposure to Malay and Indian cuisine, Singapore and Malaysian Chinese like their dishes spicier than their original versions. The local version of Hainanese chicken rice is an example. The dish originated on Hainan Island in southern China, but the Singapore and Malaysia version differs from the original through the use of the local ingredients such as the *pandan* leaf for flavoring the rice as well as hot chili sauce, minced ginger, and dark soy sauce as condiments. The love of chili is so dominant that almost all local Chinese dishes are served with some sort of hot condiment, which may be a sauce of cut chili and soy sauce or *sambal belachan* (chili with shrimp paste).

Indian

There are two main regional styles of Indian cuisine in Singapore and Malaysia: northern and southern Indian. Although the two styles of cuisine use similar spices, such as coriander, cumin, fennel, and cloves, northern Indian dishes are considerably milder. A similarity between the two is that neither contains beef, as Hindus regard the cow as a sacred animal. A number of Hindus are vegetarians. There is also a substantial Indian Muslim community whose food stalls are often patronized by Malay-Muslims.

Typical northern Indian food include Tandoori baked meats, chicken and thick curries enriched with yogurt or cream and eaten with a variety of breads such as the flat *chappati,* and the tandoor-baked *naan.* South Indian food is fiery but more commonly found in Singapore and Malaysia. In contrast to its northern cousin, southern Indian food is more rice-based, with curries enriched with coconut milk. Southern Indian cuisine also has its own breads. The dish known as *roti prata* in Singapore and *roti canai* in Malaysia—a griddle-fried flaky white-flour bread served with a thin curry sauce—is a firm favorite.

This *roti,* usually served with a curry dipping sauce, is popular among all ethnic groups and has been the object of some innovation. Traditionally served plain, it is now available as *roti prata* with fillings such as cheese, banana, or chocolate. *Dosai,* pancakes made with ground rice and lentils, are also common fare. The most impressive is the paper *dosai,* which is made extra large and as thin as a sheet of paper; it is presented like a roll of brown paper or twisted into a huge cone and is eaten with various condiments such as yogurt and *dhal* (curry made from lentils or other pulses).

Traditionally, Indian food is eaten by hand. For south Indians, a banana leaf serves as a dinner plate in the popular "banana leaf restaurants." Here, each customer gets a leaf with a scoop of rice surrounded by vegetable, *dhal,* curries, *papadam* (thin crisp bread flavored with pepper and spices), yogurt, and *rasam* (pepper water). It is also where customers go for fish head curry, an Indian-inspired local concoction of a whole fish head cooked in a spicy and sour curry.

Peranakan

Peranakan food is best eaten in the former Straits Settlements—Singapore, Malacca, and Penang, where one can still find the food prepared the traditional way. Typically the preparation of Peranakan food is laborious, as traditional dishes were designed to be complex to show off the cooking skills of the *nonya.* An example of an elaborate dish is the *kueh pie ti,* a delicate vegetable salad of hand-cut bamboo shoots, turnips, and carrots served in individual deep-fried pastry cups. The complexity of the cuisine is the reason Peranakan food is highly prized.

The Peranakan cuisine, like Peranakan culture and customs, is an intriguing mix of Chinese and Malay practices. The Peranakans remake Chinese and Malay dishes into unique dishes of their own. The *nonya* dish of *babi pong tay,* for example, is similar to the Chinese dish *tau yew bak* (pork belly slow-braised in garlic and soy sauce). The Peranakan version, however, is infused with more flavor with the addition of salted soybeans, cinnamon, and pounded shallots. Another example is the *nonya laksa,* a dish in which the Peranakans combine Chinese coarse rice noodles with a Malay-style curry. The Peranakans are also well known for their desserts, especially cakes known as *nonya kueh.* These cakes make liberal use of coconut products such as coconut milk and shredded coconut.

Eurasian

Although less famous than the cuisine of the Peranakans, the food culture of the Eurasians is unique to the region through its fusion of European,

Indian, Malay, Sri Lankan, and Chinese cuisines. There are, however, few Eurasian restaurants, as Eurasian food is mainly a home art. The dishes are intriguing adaptations of their Western counterparts. For example, instead of making a stew from leftover Christmas meats such as turkey, beef, and ham, the Eurasians make "devil curry," a delicious concoction of the meat slow-cooked with chilies, spices, and local aromatics. Another dish synonymous with the Eurasians is *sugee* cake, which is similar to a rich butter cake but uses as its main ingredients *sugee* (semolina and almonds).

TROPICAL FRUITS

A serving of tropical fruits is the most common way to end a meal in Singapore and Malaysia regardless of ethnic group. Fruits native to the region include papayas, jackfruit or *nanga* (a fragrant and sweet fruit, eaten raw or cooked in salads and curries), star fruit (so named because the cross section of the fruit resembles a five-pointed star), and *chiku* (a small round fruit with a soft texture). Fruits are sold in every market and in stalls all over Singapore and Malaysia. They are served chilled and sliced, or juiced as drinks. Some of the most popular juices are watermelon, papaya, and pineapple.

Although tropical fruit is available all year round, the seasons for some fruit are particularly anticipated. One of them is the *rambutan,* which means "hairy fruit" in Malay (it is named for its red, hairy husk). Breaking apart the husk reveals a sweet and semi-translucent flesh. Another seasonal fruit, the size of a tennis ball with a hard purple shell, is the mangosteen. When breaking open the husks, one needs to be careful because its purple juice can cause permanent stains on one's clothes. The mangosteen, considered the "queen of fruits," is in season at the same time as the durian, and it is regarded as a natural antidote to the richness of the durian.

The durian is undisputedly the most popular fruit in Singapore and Malaysia, earning it the title of the "king of fruits." It is easily recognizable by its green, spiky husk and its pungent smell. The interior of the durian is segmented, with its seeds surrounded by a rich, creamy flesh of custard-like consistency. The colors of the flesh range from light to deep rich yellow, depending on the species. According to a local saying, the durian "has the smell from hell and a taste from heaven." Singaporean and Malaysians are known to pay exorbitant sums or to travel far distances for the best-quality durians. Aside from eating them fresh, they use durians as an additive to a large variety of cakes, desserts, and sweets. Despite the locals' love of the fruit, the durian is forbidden on all public transport—trains, buses, and taxis—because its lingering smell is considered offensive to many.

Durians, the king of fruits. Courtesy of the author.

Eating Out

The culture of eating out is deeply ingrained in Singapore and the urban areas of Malaysia. The origins of this practice can be traced to the 19th century, when immigrants first streamed into the region in large numbers. As most immigrants were single males who worked long hours, they were dependent on hawkers—mobile food sellers—for quick, cheap, and tasty meals. Even though many of these migrants eventually settled down and started families of their own, they never lost their love of street food. A 2007 Singapore survey revealed that more than 90 percent of respondents eat hawker food at least once a week.[1]

Food Stalls and Centers

Street hawkers are a prominent feature of the Singapore and Malaysia food scene. Historically, these mobile food sellers hawked their products on the streets and in the villages. They used to carry their wares—crockery, stools, and the like—with them in wooden crates slung at both ends of a pole and carried on their shoulders or in push carts. Many of them also set up stalls on the streets where they sold a wide range of food from the various ethnic groups. In Malaysia, many hawkers continue to operate from mobile pushcarts or stalls in back lanes and alleys. Certain streets, such as Penang's Gurney Drive and Kuala Lumpur's Jalan Bukit Bintang, have developed reputations as "food paradises." While hygiene is sometimes a concern, there is a charm to this form of al fresco dining, which continues to be popular with local and tourists.

Since the 1970s, Singapore has relocated its street hawkers to permanent structures known as "hawker centers" as part of efforts to improve the standard of hygiene and streetscape. A hawker center is typically a large, open-air complex that can house more than 100 stalls. There is a common seating area, and customers are free to order food from any stall. These centers provide food hawkers with proper amenities and sanitation such as electricity and sewage and drainage systems. Ironically, in recent years, street hawking has been reintroduced in selected areas in Singapore, such as Smith Street in Chinatown, mainly as tourist attractions.

While hawker centers continue to be well patronized, a modern version—the food court—has emerged in recent years. Like the hawker center, food courts offer a variety of relatively low-priced food sold in separate stalls. Unlike the hawker centers, the food courts are air conditioned and clean, with attractive décor; they offer international cuisines (such as Korean, Japanese,

Street hawkers, such as this one selling claypot rice, are prominent features of the Singapore and Malaysia food scene. One can still find street hawkers in cities and towns across Malaysia, while in Singapore street vendors are much more regulated. Courtesy of the author.

and Western food), making them an attractive alternative to the hot and noisy hawker centers. Food courts can be found all over Singapore and Malaysia and are often located in shopping malls.

The Coffee Shop (Kopitiam)

The coffee shop or *kopitiam*, as it is also known, is the local version of the café and pub. There is one on every other street corner, and regulars go there not only to have their daily cup of coffee but also to meet friends and exchange the gossip of the day. In contrast to the Western franchises such as Starbucks or Gloria Jean's, which have become regular features in the newer shopping malls, the traditional coffee shop is typically a non-air-conditioned informal space with a counter at which to buy drinks and three or four stalls selling cooked food.

As at Starbucks, one may order different types of coffee such as a cappuccino or a latte, but to get the right brew in the traditional coffee shop one needs to be acquainted with the local lingo. Local coffee with sugar and condensed milk is known as *kopi,* and coffee with sugar but no milk is known as *kopi-O.* Besides coffee, the *kopitiam* serves a wide range of beverages such as tea and soft drinks, as well as breakfast food. The traditional breakfast served is typically coffee with a pair of soft-boiled eggs and *kaya* toast. The *kaya* toast consists of two slices of charcoal-toasted bread bonded by a thick spread of butter and *kaya* (coconut jam flavored with pandan leaves).

The *kopitiam* has been given a modern revamp in recent years to better appeal to the younger generation of Singaporeans and Malaysians. Many of them are now operated as modern franchise outlets with stylish décor, air conditioning, and even wireless Internet access. In addition to traditional coffees and food, they are also likely to serve Western-style café food such as French toast and iced blended coffees.

Fast-food Chains and Restaurants

With globalization, the range of cuisines available in Singapore and Malaysia has increased tremendously. On one hand there are the American fast-food restaurants such as McDonald's, Burger King, Pizza Hut, and Kentucky Fried Chicken, which have numerous outlets in Singapore and Malaysia. While many locals now enjoy eating burgers, french fries, and fried chicken, these Western fast-food chains have also adapted their menus to suit local taste. For example, many of these fast-food restaurants use pork substitutes rather than the traditional bacon and ham in their food to cater to Malays who abstain from pork. Burger King, for example, uses turkey bacon for its popular bacon cheeseburger. The outlets also serve East-West innovations such as the *rendang* burger, in which a burger patty is drenched in *rendang* sauce (*rendang* is a popular Malay beef curry dish).

Besides the Western-style fast food, there is a wide range of international cuisine available in Singapore and Malaysia, such as Japanese, Korean, Thai, Vietnamese, Italian, and French, just to name a few. East Asian cuisine in the form of Japanese sushi and Korean barbeque are very popular, as is Italian pasta and pizza. It used to be that one could sample such cuisine only in expensive restaurants, but more affordable versions are now easily available in informal cafés and food courts. International cuisine is a favorite theme of many food courts, and some in Malaysia are even *halal* to enable patronage by the Malay community.

With increasing wealth in the region, there has been a corresponding growth in the number of high-end restaurants. Gourmet food and wine are new trends among the well-heeled in Singapore and Malaysia. The two countries now have a range of fine-dining restaurants and host annual gourmet food festivals, which are discussed in Chapter 8.

TRADITIONAL ETHNIC COSTUMES

Although Western dress is popular for everyday wear, traditional ethnic costumes are still worn on festive occasions such as New Year celebrations and on formal occasions such as weddings. Ethnic costumes are also an essential component of traditional dance and theater performances. With modernization, some elements of these costumes have undergone change, such as the use of more convenient factory-made products and technologies.

Indigenous Tribes

Traditional costumes are important for the cultural identity of indigenous tribes because they serve as a means of distinguishing the tribes from one another. In addition, elaborate costumes are often a critical part of the tribes' religious ceremonies and rituals. The ceremonial costumes of the Dusun Tindal tribe of Sabah are a case in point. Women wear black velvet blouses with slashed sleeves flared at the elbow with gold trimming, dyed skirts with embroidered hems, sashes made of *kain dastar,* and accessories such as silver necklaces, belts, and bangles. The costume for men is similar except that a shirt and trousers are worn instead of the blouse and skirt. There is great variation in the designs of tribal costumes, which are highly dependent on the expertise of the particular tribe in beading, weaving, or silversmithing.

Tribal costumes traditionally made from materials taken from the immediate natural environment have been affected by modernity and Westernization.

Textiles that were once hand woven have been replaced by machine-woven cloth; ornaments such as gemstones, glass beds, shells, and bronze pieces have been replaced by items incorporating more modern materials such as plastic, gold and silver threads, and sequins. The conversion of many tribal people to Christianity and Islam has also meant that some costumes have to be adopted to take into account new conceptions of modesty. Last, the growth of tourism has had both positive and negative effects. On one hand, the increasing number of tourists to tribal longhouses serves as an incentive for tribes to preserve traditional dress and performance. On the other hand, the need to impress tourists has motivated tribes to embellish these costumes to make them more attractive to the tourist gaze.

Malay

The traditional costume of the Malay community is the *baju Melayu* or *baju kurung,* as it is commonly referred to in Singapore. In Malaysia, the *baju Melayu* is also the country's national costume to be worn for all official functions. It is also the official attire for Malay royalty, although the material and design of royal garments are superior to those made for common wear. Yellow, the color reserved for royalty, often features prominently in such official *baju*s. The *baju* is a dress, shirt, or tunic that covers the upper part of the body. Often it is a long-sleeved tunic with a circular neckline and a short vent opening to allow the garment to be pulled over the head. More formal *baju*s come with mandarin collars of around 1.5 inches in height. The *baju* is usually worn over a *sarong,* which is a loose garment made up of a long strip of cloth and wrapped around the lower part of the body, akin to a wrap skirt. Very often, the men wear the *baju* with a pair of pants (*seluar*). On more formal occasions, the men wear a *kain samping* at the waist. The *kain samping* is a colorful piece of handwoven fabric with an elaborate design. A modern alternative to the *baju kurung* is the *batik* shirt paired with dark-colored trousers.

Many Malay women also wear the *baju kurung* as daily wear because it is loose and comfortable, especially in the tropical heat of Singapore and Malaysia. The *baju*s are usually made of cotton or cotton mixed with polyester. For festive occasions, women often wear *baju*s made by tailors, with more elaborate designs and made of more expensive material, such as silk. Younger Malay women may however, prefer the *sarong kebaya,* which is a form-fitting top paired with a sarong skirt, as they feel it is more flattering than the loose-fitting *baju.* In recent years, Malay women have started to wear other ethnic costumes that meet their modesty requirements, such as the *ao dai,* the Vietnamese national costume, comprising a long top with a Mandarin collar and pants.

Malay men sometimes wear a *songkok,* the traditional Malay headgear that resembles a brimless cap. The hat can be made from cotton or velvet, and designs range from plain black to *batik* prints. Some of the more elaborate *songkoks* have embroidery, and these are often worn during festive, formal, or religious occasions. A white *songkok* is worn by a man who has performed the *haj* to Mecca, while black *songkoks* are the most common.

The growth of fundamentalist Islam in Malaysia in the 1980s has influenced fashion styles, especially among Muslim women. Islam's strict modesty rules require women to cover all parts of their bodies except for their hands and faces. Many Malay-Muslim women in Singapore and Malaysia, particularly in the Islamic strongholds of northern Malaysia, wear *tudungs* (headscarves) with the traditional *baju kurung.* There is a wide variety of *tudung* designs, ranging from the highly sequinned and beaded or floral patterned to plain black.

Chinese

The majority of Chinese in Singapore and Malaysia were historically peasants from southern China, whose traditional clothes were plain and simple. Chinese laborers, or coolies, usually wore comfortable, loose-fitting pants and a simple shirt or a thin, white singlet, while the women did their work in a *samfu. Sam* is a generic term used to refer to an upper garment, which is usually a top with a mandarin collar and sleeves of varying lengths. The garment has an asymmetrical front opening sloping toward the right underarm that is fastened either by Chinese frog buttons or by metallic press studs, or snaps. Over time, many women started wearing the *sam* tighter and the sleeves shorter, which was considered to be more flattering. The sam was worn with a *fu,* a pair of loose straight trousers of ankle length. The *samfu* was usually made from the same material, projecting a sense of unity of design. The material used varied depending on the finances of the wearer.

As the Chinese became wealthier, they began to adopt the fashion of the Chinese elite, such as long silk tunics, buttoned at the neck, with silk trousers for the men and the *cheongsam* for the women. The term *cheongsam* was originally a generic term used to mean a loose-fitting long dress that could be worn by both men and women. Men often wore it with a pair of trousers and women with a long skirt. By the 20th century, the *cheongsam* evolved into a figure-hugging high-collared dress with cap sleeves. The dress had two side slits (the most daring reached up to the thighs), and the hem fell just below the knee. The *cheongsam* is made of silk or brocade and is worn on special occasions, as it is too restrictive for everyday wear.

The Chinese community is perhaps the one that has most readily abandoned traditional ways of dressing in favor of modern trends. Yet, the glamorous *cheongsam* is a still popular option for the Chinese New Year and for formal occasions. Traditional costume also makes an appearance during the tea ceremony of a Chinese wedding. Although the groom is usually in a Western suit, many Chinese brides don the traditional *kwa,* a two-piece outfit, typically red and decorated with gold and silver embroidery with dragon and phoenix motifs. The Chinese also continue to be conscious of cultural fashion norms that encourage the wearing of bright and 'lucky' colors such as red and orange for the Chinese New Year and avoiding them for mournful occasions such as funerals. It is also still regarded as taboo to be dressed top to toe in black—no matter how chic it may be—for happy occasions such as wedding celebrations.

Peranakan

The traditional costume of the Peranakans borrows liberally from the Malay and Chinese styles in a somewhat eclectic manner. Male Peranakans (*babas*), however, tended to favor either traditional European or Chinese wear. Those with English education prefer British ways of dressing—tie, shirt, jacket, and trousers—while Chinese-oriented *babas* prefer the traditional Chinese style of loose pants and Chinese-style jacket over a singlet or shirt. The traditional outfit of the Peranakan woman (*nonya*) is the *sarong kebaya,* similar to those worn by women in the Malay community. The difference is mainly in the *kebaya* (fitted top); the Perankan version is often elaborately embroidered and revealing, and is often trimmed with lace and made of sheer or translucent material, showing off a camisole underneath or, since the late 20th century, a bra. In addition, the *kebaya* is only part of an ensemble that includes matching jewelry and shoes. Given the wealth of the Peranakans, the *kebaya* top is held together not by buttons but by a set of three ornate gold brooches, often with embedded diamonds or precious stones (*kerosang*); the *batik sarong* is held together by a silver linked belt, This outfit is combined with hand-beaded slippers known as *kasut manek.*

Over time, the *sarong kebaya* has been updated for convenience. The beautiful *kerosangs* on the *kebaya* have been replaced by press studs and the silver belt by a waistband and zipper on the *sarong.* Unlike the *kebayas* of old, which were handmade and expensive, the modern versions are more reasonably priced, although far less intricate. Even as the numbers of *nonyas* wearing the traditional dress has decreased, the outfit has grown in popularity among the larger population of Malays and Chinese. It is common to see modern women wear the *kebaya* or beaded shoes with jeans or slacks in their own interpretation of Peranakan dress. The form-fitting style of the *sarong kebaya* was the inspiration for the uniforms of the air stewardesses on the national airlines of Singapore and Malaysia.

Indians

The traditional dress of the southern Indians is the *dhoti* for the men and the *sari* for the women, both of which are basically a length of unsewn material used for draping. The *dhoti* is a lower garment for men draped to form front pleats. It is usually worn with a shirt or *kurta* (a loose long-sleeved shirt) or nothing at all. The *sari* is essentially a piece of cloth, about 6 to 9 yards in length, wrapped around the waist several times and then draped over the shoulders. *Sari* material comes in numerous vibrant colors that complement the dark complexion of the Indians, and one can tell that a cloth is meant for a *sari* by its decorative gold borders. It is usually worn with a short, tight blouse known as the *choli,* whose styles change with fashion trends. For example, the *choli* in the early 20th century had a high neckline and long sleeves, but since the 1960s it has become shorter, with sleeves ending above the elbow and the *choli* itself ending above the navel. Wealthier Indian women also typically wear the *sari* with loads of gold jewelry in the form of intricate and elaborate hair pieces, earrings, necklaces, and wrist and ankle bangles.

Although the Indians in Singapore and Malaysia tend to be divided along north-south lines, these lines are blurred when it comes to ethnic costumes. The southern Indians, who are in the majority, also wear a northern-influenced blouse and pant combination, the *salwar kameez,* also known as the Punjabi suit, because of its greater practicality. The *salwars* are drawstring pants, usually narrow at the ankle, while the *kameez* is a long tunic with side seams usually left open below the waistline. Both men and women wear the *salwar kameez,* but women also wear a *salwar kameez dupatta* ensemble (the *dupatta* is a long scarf that can be draped across the woman's head and across her shoulders). Elaborate decorative patterns are often embroidered around the neckline, sleeves, and hems of the tunic and trousers. This outfit can be casual or formal depending on the material and the handwork of the suit.

FASHION TODAY

Western fashion has been popular in Singapore and Malaysia since the mid-20th century and is dominant in everyday fashion. Office workers are often in tailored outfits, although the warm weather often makes a full suit impractical. The standard outfit for men consists of tailored pants, a long-sleeved shirt, and a tie. Women tend to wear office suits and dresses. Outside work, the ubiquitous T-shirts and jeans or bermudas (shorts that reach down to the knee) are the preferred attire. The influence of Western dress is perhaps more muted among the Malays because of Islam's modesty requirements, yet the modern Muslim woman is still fashionably dressed. Despite wearing a headscarf that completely covers her hair, she drapes the scarf beautifully and often expertly matches it with the colors and patterns of her *baju kurung,* shoes, handbag, and accessories. It is also common to see young Muslim girls don the *tudong* with long-sleeved T-shirts, blue jeans, and high heels.

Singaporeans and Malaysians are influenced more than ever by global consumer fashion and its trends. This is especially so in Singapore and the larger cities of Malaysia. A glance at the local fashion magazines shows that urban folk take their fashion cues from Hollywood stars and the catwalks of Paris and Milan. There is often a sense that overseas fashions, even if they are not specifically designed with the local climate in mind, are considered superior to locally designed and made clothes.

This is especially so for Singapore, which is still struggling to develop its local fashion industry and even a national costume. Unlike Malaysia, which has the *baju Melayu* as its official national costume, Singapore is still grappling to develop one. The debate over the national costume has persisted over several decades, most often prompted by Singapore's participation in the Miss Universe contests and the need for participants to wear a national costume. While Miss China parades confidently in a *cheongsam* and Miss Vietnam in an *ao dai,* Miss Singapore often appears in some three-in-one monstrosity that combines Chinese, Malay, and Indian motifs. In the late 1990s, there was a move to design an official "Singapore dress" for official functions. While many designers submitted suggestions along the lines of the three-in-one concept, these were all rejected in favor of an orchid motif, based on Singapore's national flower, the Vanda Miss Joaquim orchid. The orchid motif, found on ties, shirts, and blouses, has become somewhat representative of the Singapore dress. Despite its endorsement by ministers and government official, the orchid motif has yet to catch on with the general public.

NOTE

1. See Lily Kong, *Singapore Hawker Centres: People, Places, Food* (Singapore: National Environment Agency, 2007), p. 104.

SUGGESTED READING

Chan, Margaret. *Margaret Chan's Foodstops.* Singapore: Landmark Books, 1992.

Costumes Through Time. Singapore: National Heritage Board and Fashion Design Society, 1993.

Garrett, Valery M. *Traditional Chinese Clothing.* Hong Kong: Oxford University Press, 1987.

Hutton, Wendy. *Singapore Food.* Singapore: Marshall Cavendish, 2007.

Kong, Lily. *Singapore Hawker Centres: People, Places, Food.* Singapore: National Environment Agency, 2007.

Lasimbang, Rita, and Stella Moo-Tan. *An Introduction to the Traditional Costumes of Saba.,* Kota Kinabalu: Natural History Publications in association with the Department of Sabah Museum, 1997.

Mohd Ismail Noor. (ed.). *The Food of ASEAN.* Kuala Lumpur: ASEAN Committee on Culture and Information, 2000.

Tan, Su-Lyn. *Lonely Planet World Food Malaysia and Singapore.* Footscray, Victoria, BC: Lonely Planet, 2003.

7

Gender, Courtship, Marriage, and Family

SINGAPORE AND MALAYSIA are progressing toward greater gender equality, although men continue to dominate the public spheres of government and economy. Various women's groups that have been set up since independence have been campaigning for women's voices to be heard. The family continues to be regarded as the basic unit of society, as reflected in the importance ascribed to the institutions of marriage and childbirth. Among the main demographic challenges are declining birth rates, which both governments are trying to arrest.

Tensions between the old and the new feature prominently in the issues of gender, marriage, and family in modern Singapore and Malaysia. Traditions dictate that old ways and mentalities remain, while modernization wants to leave traditions behind. This gives rise to contradictions. For example, while it is now common to find well-educated, professional, and single women in modern societies as such Singapore's and Malaysia's, there are still pressures for them to marry and have children. And, while many young couples may want to have a simple and romantic wedding, they have to fight against their parents' wish for a huge banquet for hundreds of friends and business acquaintances. These tensions and contradictions have shaped and will continue to influence the status of women, the kind of courtship, marriage, and family life in Singapore and Malaysia. Religion, especially Islam, still has a large influence on the roles of Muslim women and family in both countries.

ROLE OF MEN AND WOMEN IN SOCIETY

In the two countries, men were traditionally esteemed over women because they were the breadwinners and, in some cases, better educated. Traditional gender roles dictated that men should work and bring home the bacon, while the women should stay at home to take care of domestic matters, such as rearing children and doing household chores. But, with social changes, the roles of men and women also began to shift, narrowing the gender divide. As their opportunities for education expanded, women could work in areas that were traditionally men's domain, such as medicine and banking. The growing economies of the two countries also opened the door for women to participate more actively in the economy because of the need to expand the labor force. Women are now an important economic force, working in a range of jobs in offices, factories, and shops. This, however, does not mean a change in the traditional role of the women; the domestic sphere is still considered the natural responsibility of the women. In addition to their professional roles, most women are still expected to be responsible for the home, even though many modern families now employ live-in domestic maids.

Legally, women in Singapore and Malaysia enjoy equal status with men. They have voting rights, are able to own and trade property, and own and operate businesses. Almost half of Singapore and Malaysia's labor force is made up of women.[1] In Singapore, the rights of women are enshrined in the Women's Charter, a legislative act that is also the legal basis for equality between husband and wife. Passed in 1961, the Women's Charter grants equal rights and duties to both husbands and wives in domestic affairs. Under the Charter, polygamy is outlawed, and husbands are obliged to provide for their wives and children during marriage and after divorce. The outlawing of polygamy was significant as the practice was historically well accepted in Chinese and Malay communities. Today, polygamy is still allowed in Islamic law, although it is not as widespread as it used to be. The divorced spouse is entitled to a share of matrimonial assets. Offenses against women and girls, such as rape or pimping, are punishable. In addition to legislation, women's rights are also promoted by the Association of Women for Action and Research (AWARE). Its goal, since its inception in 1985, is to promote the understanding of gender equality and to bring related issues to the forefront to be debated and worked on.

The importance of women's issues in Malaysia has been gaining ground in the past few decades. Since 1975, various councils and secretariats at the national level have been established to handle women's issues. Many of these units, shuffled over the years between the prime minister's department and the Ministry of National Unity and Social Development, were tasked with promoting and encouraging women's involvement in the country's development. Although there was an initial plan for a Ministry of Women's Affairs in 2001, the agency's agenda was later expanded to include the functions of the national family planning board and furthering social development. The new ministry eventually became the Ministry of Women, Family, and Community Development, established in 2007. These developments reflect the social perception that a woman's role is inevitably tied to the family and community.

In Malaysia, there are also several nongovernmental organizations dedicated to advancing and protecting women's rights. Much of their work revolves around educating women on issues of domestic and sexual violence, as well as on women's rights in general. Many of them also advocate for the right of Muslim women especially to be governed by legislative acts, rather than being subjected to the jurisdiction of the Syariah Court, which deals with all matters relating to marriage, divorce, and property allocation for Muslims. As mentioned in Chapter 1, all Muslims in Malaysia are also subject to Islamic law (Syariah). One of the leading campaigners for women's rights in Malaysia is Marina Mahathir, daughter of the country's former prime minister Mahathir Mohammad. She is also actively involved in raising awareness of HIV-AIDS in the country.

In the decades since the two countries' independence, women in Singapore and Malaysia have become very prominent in the economic sector. The active participation of women in the labor force is very much a result of economic necessity. Many working-class and middle-class families need two incomes to ensure that their needs are met, especially with the increasing standards of living. Many women are found in traditionally women-dominated jobs such as nurses, teachers, and office clerks. Increasing, however, many women are now doctors, lawyers, and even judges. The increasing number of women in the workforce is also a result of the increasing opportunities for education and professional advancement. Among the most prominent business leaders in Singapore is Ho Ching, chief executive officer of Temasek Holdings, the investment arm of the Singapore government. A graduate of Stanford University, Ho was on the *Forbes* list of the most powerful women (outside the United States) for several years. In 2007, she was also named by *Time* magazine as among the "100 most influential men and women" who shaped the world. Another prominent female business leader in Singapore is Jannie Tay, vice chairman of the luxury watch company The Hour Glass. In addition to holding management positions in various business organizations, Tay is also active in several charitable and social organizations.

In contrast to the private sector, fewer women are active in government and politics. There are only a handful of women in the top echelons of politics in Singapore and Malaysia. In 2008, only 23 out of Singapore's 94 parliamentarians were female, and there were no female cabinet ministers. In Malaysia, only 40 out of 279 parliamentarians were women; there were only 2 female cabinet ministers. There has been much debate on the issue of women ministers and leaders; most people argue for greater representation of women in the political realm. While this is ideal, others argue that this is asking too much of women, who are expected to be mothers, wives, and workers on top of having additional public duties. The few women in government have, however, made a strong impact. In Malaysia, for example, former cabinet minister Rafidah Aziz was the country's most prominent female politician, holding the position of Minister of International Trade and Industry for 20 years, starting in 1987. She was also the head of the ruling United Malays National Organization's Woman Wing (Wanita UMNO in Malay). More recently, Wan Azizah Ismail and Nurul Izzah Anwar—the wife and daughter, respectively, of opposition politician Anwar Ibrahim–have risen to prominence in Malaysian politics. Wan Azizah headed the political party Keadilan after her husband was dismissed as Malaysia's deputy prime minister and arrested by the authorities. She is now the party's president. Her daughter, 27-year-old Nurul Izzah, an engineer by training and a Johns Hopkins University graduate, was elected to the Parliament in 2008.

COURTSHIP AND DATING

Marriage is a major milestone in one's life, as it symbolizes the attainment of adulthood, and one's responsibilities are increased accordingly. Because marriage is seen as a joining of two families, parents and family elders are frequently involved in the nuptial decision making. Sometimes this includes the choice of spouse. Arranged marriages were once common in Singapore and Malaysia. Almost every ethnic community has its equivalent of a matchmaker, usually a professional or a family elder. Appointed by the family, the matchmaker plays Cupid, searching for or appraising a compatible match for the children of marriageable age. Getting a right match was seen as important for harmonious ties or family advancement; children were considered too young and ignorant of what was good for them to pick their own spouses, creating the need for matchmakers.

But, with Western influence, ideas of romance and love have caught hold. More often than not, the young now choose whom to date. It is not uncommon to see young students holding hands, sometimes still in their uniforms. Valentine's Day is now widely celebrated; roses, chocolates, and cute gifts go on sale as early as six weeks prior. During the period, newspapers, radio, and television print and broadcast declarations of love while couples have candlelit dinners in restaurants.

Although most marriages today are a result of personal rather than familial choices, there are still communities—such as the Malays and the Indians—that still practice some form of matchmaking. This is largely a result of the influence of the religion. Orthodox Islam, for example, discourages contact between single individuals of the opposite sex without a chaperone. This makes it hard for many youngsters to date romantically. The Malays still uses the "*tukang risik*" (literally "spy"), a traditional matchmaker. The family usually asks the *tukang risik* to scout around for a compatible match for its children. The "recommended" individuals are introduced to each other, who then "date" (usually with a chaperone) to see if they like each other enough to move the relationship toward marriage. Although love-marriages are on the rise in the Indian community, arranged marriages remain a strong preference. Anecdotal evidence suggests that there are more cases of arranged marriages among the Indians than in other ethnic communities. Families enlist the help of family friends or respected elders of the community to act as matchmakers to find suitable partners for the children. Many Indian families that maintain strong ties in India, also arrange trips back to their home villages to scout for potential partners for their children.

Although matchmaking is seen as old-fashioned, a modern form of matchmaking in the form of dating agencies has become increasingly popular in Singapore and Malaysia in recent years. While most young Singaporeans and Malaysians want to find their own partners, many are too busy with their working life to do so. Dating agencies usually target busy executives who might otherwise not have the opportunities to enlarge their social circles. These agencies organize various activities such as speed-dating and lunch and dinner dates as the initial meetings. One dating agency in Singapore even organized a public session where parents with unmarried children met to exchange photos and information about their children in the hope of securing them a partner. In this age of technology, many single Singaporeans and Malaysians have also turned to the Internet to search for potential partners on dating Web sites or in chat rooms. A recent trend among some of the older Chinese men, usually bachelors or widowers, is to find wives through marriage agencies. Many of the agencies introduce and match foreign women, usually from Vietnam, China, or Indonesia, to the local men and even arrange for wedding packages for the couples. Most of the men who turn to such marriage agencies have found local women to be more demanding in their expectations and less pliable than women from other countries in the region.

In Singapore, even the government has gotten into the matchmaking act. In 1984 and 1985, the government set up the Social Development Unit and the Social Development Service respectively as matchmakers for graduate and nongraduate Singaporeans. Although both units cater to different groups of Singaporeans, the objective was similar—to encourage young Singaporeans to get married or at least to provide the opportunities for those who want to get married. Activities such as dancing, sports, workshops, seminars, dinners, camping, and overseas trips were organized. Although the SDU is still under the auspices of the Ministry of Community, Youth and Sport, it is now a fully privatized agency.

Despite increased interaction among the various ethnic groups in Singapore and Malaysia, interethnic marriages are still not common. Among some of the most frequently voiced objections include the difference in religion and culture. For example, all non-Muslims who marry Muslims are required to convert to Islam and adopt the Islamic culture. This is often a barrier to members of the non-Muslim communities, which, with the exception of some of the more fervent Christians, do not require their spouses to convert to their religion. For Chinese families, especially, this also affects more trivial aspects of life such as the eating of pork or the drinking of alcohol, both of which are prohibited by Islam but are the mainstays of Chinese cuisine. Some objections to interethnic marriages, however, are more superficial, such as concerns over skin color or the "mixed" appearances of the children from such marriages. Very often, it is the families that are more resistant to such interethnic arrangements than the couples themselves.

GETTING MARRIED

Wedding ceremonies in all ethnic groups are often elaborate and colorful affairs. While the specific rites and rituals concerning marriage are different for each ethnic group, the main stages of the wedding are similar. These stages include the preparation period before the wedding, the wedding ceremony itself, and the feast or celebration that follows.

Malays

The Malay wedding is a bright, colorful, and noisy affair; one can often tell that a wedding is taking place by the sight of the *bunga manggar* (palm blossom) and the rousing beats of the *kompang,* a traditional Malay drum made from goat- or cowhide. Such festivities are often features of the wedding day (*bersanding*). On this day, the groom is accompanied by a *kompang* band, *bunga manggar* carriers, friends, and relatives to the bride's place. There is usually a playful delay at the bride's place, with a group of the bride's female friends and younger relatives trying to stop the groom from reaching the bride. The groom usually has to "pay" his way with a symbolic present of money. Once the bride is fetched, the couple then returns to the groom's house, where the couple may be welcomed with traditional Malay martial arts or dances.

Like many major festivities, the actual wedding day is preceded by a flurry of preparations. It is still customary for the groom's representative, usually an elderly male relative, to ask for the hand of the bride from her family. A small entourage usually accompanies the groom's representative, bearing gifts for the bride's family. The tradition includes requesting the bride's hand in poetic exchanges of Malay verses. Once the bride's family has agreed, dates for the engagement and the wedding are set. An *imam* (religious leader) conducts the solemnization of the marriage (*akad nikah*) on the eve of the wedding. During the *akad nikah,* the groom signs the marriage contract and agrees to provide the bride with a *mas kahwin* (dowry). The *mas kahwin* is given by the groom to the bride to symbolize the beginning of his responsibilities in providing for the wife. It is usually cash but can also be in the form of land, property, a car, silver or gold, or other valuables. The marriage is confirmed once the couple takes the vow.

The actual wedding day is known as *bersanding,* which literally means the "sitting together of the bride and bridegroom on the bridal couch." The bridal couch is known as the *pelamin* and is the centerpiece of the wedding day. The bridal couple, regarded as king and queen for the day, sits on the *pelamin* on a raised platform. They are then sprinkled with yellow rice and scented water by family members, relatives, and guests as a sign of blessing. At the end of the *bersanding* is the celebratory feast. In Singapore, this is usually held at the void deck (a plaza-like space on the ground floor) of a housing block or, in the case of Malaysia, in any open space in the village or housing estate. The reception is a relatively informal gathering of friends and family, who do not necessarily have to stay for the whole duration of the feast. Usually, guests have some food and chat with other guests. Before leaving, they usually present a gift of money to the couple, with the amount given dependent on the guests' financial abilities and their relationship with the couple. In the past, it was not unusual for guests to bring various dishes to the reception, much like for a large-scale potluck party. This has been replaced by professional catering, with the food being prepared on the spot and easily replenished. A Malay band is usually hired to add to the festive occasion. These days, karaoke, in which the guests perform their favorite songs to taped musical accompaniment, is becoming a common entertainment for the wedding day.

Malay couples are treated like kings and queens on their wedding day. Courtesy of the author.

Chinese

The lights in the hotel ballroom dim, and a hush falls over the packed room of several hundred people. The bridal couple walks in on a red carpet laid in the center of the ballroom to the tune of the *Bridal Chorus* and applause from the audience. After they are seated, a brief silence ensues before the theme song from the *Indiana Jones* movies is blared over the speakers and the spotlight falls on the door. In a split second, the doors burst open again, and a troop of smartly dressed waiters and waitresses balancing plates on their hands emerge amid simulated mist and make their way to the numerous tables. On cue, they set the food down and invite the guests to enjoy what will be the first dish of the night. During the dinner, the couple usually thank their parents and toasts to the guests.

This is what happens at most Chinese wedding dinners in Singapore and Malaysia. The dinner marks the conclusion of the day and is one of a series of carefully planned events. The dinner is not just a time for feasting; it is also for "showing off," with specially planned slideshows or creative short films documenting the couple's journey of love. Very often, the scale and the expense incurred for the dinner are used to reflect the status of the couple and their families—the more guests invited and the higher the cost, the more prestigious it is for the family, usually the parents. The banquet is usually an eight- or nine-course dinner held at a Chinese restaurant or at a hotel. Unlike the free-and-easy atmosphere of the Malay wedding reception, the Chinese dinner reception is more formal. Guests dress up and bring gifts of *ang pows* (red packets containing money) for the newlyweds. The dinner usually lasts for about two to three hours, with rowdy games and toasts to the couple in between courses.

Whether matchmade or not, Chinese couples still follow some traditional rituals when it comes to weddings. Usually, months ahead of the wedding, the couple's families meet to discuss details relating to the date, dowry, and wedding banquet. The Chinese community in both Singapore and Malaysia are often picky about wedding dates. While some still consult the almanac for auspicious dates, many couples—including the more modern ones—often jump at the chance for the wedding to take place on "special" dates, such as September 19, 1999. The number 9 sounds like the Cantonese word for "long," and that particular date is seen to be auspicious as it symbolizes a long-lasting marriage. Other popular dates include June 6 and August 8. According to Chinese belief, June 6, or "lok" in Cantonese, sounds like "luck," while 8 represents prosperity; dates with double 6s or double 8s are therefore considered auspicious dates to marry. On days like this, increasingly including Valentine's Day for its connotation of romance, the wedding registries see a record number of couples registering to get married. In Malaysia, mass weddings on special dates are common.

In some of the more traditional families, there is an exchange of three traditional letters (the betrothal letter to formally request for the hand in marriage, the gift letter that accompanies the exchanges of gifts, and the wedding letter, which officially accepts the bride into the family) and of six etiquettes (proposal, divination of birth dates, confirmation, presentation of gifts, choosing of wedding date, and acceptance of marriage) between the two families. It is also fashionable for the couple to have a photo shoot, usually a few months before the wedding, at different locations for their wedding album. The album is a keepsake for the couple, but it is also often displayed at the wedding reception for guests to view.

On the day of the wedding, the groom heads to the bride's home to fetch her, usually during an auspicious time suggested by a Chinese astrologer. As among the Malays, the groom is escorted by an entourage of male friends and relatives to the bride's place, where they have to "bribe" the bride's entourage of female friends and relatives, stationed at the door, in order to reach the bride. This activity is often boisterous, as the female entourage try to "sabotage" the groom's attempts by requesting huge amounts of cash or requiring the groom to answer tricky questions. After the groom finally reaches the bride, the couple returns to the groom's house, where the tea ceremony is conducted. If the couple practices the Chinese religion, they will first pay respects to the household deities and departed ancestors. The tea ceremony is often considered one of the most important ceremonies. Symbolically, it is the bride and groom's introduction to the family. Traditionally, the couple kneels while serving tea to their family members, in order of their status, with the eldest being served first. In return, those who were served tea give the couple an *ang pow* or jewelry as blessings. A second tea ceremony is conducted later at the bride's home with her family before the couple prepare themselves for the wedding banquet in the evening.

Modern couples often adapt these customs to their needs. Many choose not to have a traditional wedding ceremony and opt for a civil marriage at the Registry of Marriage, followed by a lunch reception. Some have chosen to totally avoid celebrations by registering their marriage before proceeding for a honeymoon overseas rather than entertaining a large number of relatives and friends at a reception or dinner. While this practice is often admired by the couple's peers, it is often frowned upon by family elders, who consider marriage a celebration for the parents as much as for the bridal couple. Although many Chinese Christian converts have church weddings, the tea ceremony and the wedding banquet are also part of their wedding celebrations.

Indian

Preparation for an Indian wedding can start as early as a year before the event. Like the Malays and Chinese, Indians choose an auspicious date for

An Indian couple decked out in their traditional costumes on their wedding day. Courtesy of Reavathi d/o Sinnathamby.

the wedding. The confirmation of the wedding date is usually done in the presence of elders or a priest. A few days before the wedding takes place, the groom's family visits the bride at her home to present her with a gift of bangles. The groom also presents a small nugget of gold to the bride, which will be smelted by a goldsmith into a *thali*, a pendant that symbolizes the binding of the couple. Before the wedding or on the day itself, the feet and hands of the couple are decorated with henna. The couple performs absolution rituals at their respective homes before they are anointed with spices, such as turmeric and sandalwood, and oil.

Traditional Hindu wedding rituals are elaborate and often involve extensive prayers and ceremonial acts. The actual wedding ceremony is held at the temple and comprises some 10 rites. These rites vary from subgroup to subgroup. Generally, the wedding ceremony begins with chanting and blessings of the groom, who arrives first with his best man, by a priest. The bride then joins the groom just after the ceremony has begun. During the ceremony, the priest unites the couple by tying a piece of cord around the bride's and groom's fingers. The *thali* and the *sari* that the groom will give to the bride are blessed by the priest. While the bride leaves to change into the new *sari*, the priest gives the garlands the bridal couple will wear to be blessed by the guests.

One of the most important rituals of the Indian wedding is the *thali*-tying ceremony, which the groom performs when the bride returns in her new *sari*. It is as significant as the Western tradition of exchanging rings at the altar. The groom ties the *thali* to the bride's neck with three knots, symbolizing the bride's promises to serve parents, God, and husband. By accepting it, the bride accepts these responsibilities, and the marriage is confirmed. After this ceremony is carried out, the guests sprinkle saffron rice as a blessing for the couple, who then exchange the garlands blessed earlier. The couple then walks three times around the ceremonial fire provided by two *kuthu-vilakku* (lamps placed on the floor), throwing a handful of grains into the fire at each circling. This is to keep the fire burning, symbolizing the eternal flame of love. As the couple circles the fire, the groom places the bride's foot on a stone and slips toe-rings onto her toes. Guests are invited to a feast after the wedding ceremony. Every community has its own traditional menu for the feast. The meal is often vegetarian, with vegetables cooked in coconut-based gravy, rice, salads, and dishes of beans, yams, potatoes, pumpkins, and carrots. The food is usually served on banana leaves. These days, some couples have opted for non-Indian cuisines for their wedding feasts, and even cocktail parties.

In the past, going through these customary rituals was sufficient to confirm the union. Now all marriages in Singapore and Malaysia, regardless of the couple's religion and ethnicity, have to be registered with the respective government agencies. In both Singapore and Malaysia, separate authorities govern Islamic and non-Islamic marriages. With exception of Islamic marriages, all civil marriages and divorces in Singapore are administered according to the Women's Charter in the courts. Muslim marriages are governed by the Islamic laws under the administration of the Syariah Court. In Malaysia, non-Islamic marriages are governed by civil and criminal laws and are registered with the National Registration Department. A Muslim marriage cannot be registered with the non-Muslim registry. All Muslim marriages must be registered with the State Religious Office and the couples must undergo a marriage course at a center certified by the State Religious Affairs Department before making their marriage application. All non-Muslims must convert to the Islamic faith before they can marry a Muslim.

In Singapore and Malaysia, monogamy is the norm. The exception is the Muslim community, as Islam permits polygamy. This practice is born out of Islam's history, in which women and children who had lost their male supporters were taken care of. Even though polygamy is allowed under Islamic laws, the number of Muslims who have multiple wives in Singapore is very small. Polygamy is an expensive affair, as Islamic law requires that the man provide for all his wives equally. Furthermore, there is growing social awareness among the younger generation that polygamy is incongruous with the modern lifestyle. Stories of abandonment and neglect have also fueled debates about the merits of polygamous relationships. In fact, the 2000 census shows about 18 percent of Muslim women in Singapore filed for divorce on the grounds of infidelity.[2] Recently, Malaysia introduced legislation that made it easier for Muslim men to take on multiple wives; men no longer need to prove their ability to financially provide for their multiple wives equally. Muslim women and women's groups have been outraged by an amendment to the bill that allows Muslim men to seize the property of their existing wives upon divorce. Under the amendment, the men also have reduced financial obligations toward their divorced wives.

DIVORCE

Although it is becoming more common, divorce remains a relative taboo in social conversations. Statistical studies reflect an increasing rate of divorce in Singapore and Malaysia.[3] Some attribute this trend to increased affluence and education, especially among women, who are now less willing to tolerate infidelity or an abusive or dysfunctional marriage. Since many women are no longer dependent on men to provide their livelihood, women are more likely to opt for divorce in such cases. Many divorcing couples also cite personality differences as a reason for going their separate ways, leading the authorities to believe that some people heading down the aisle are unprepared for marriage and therefore are more likely to bail out when they encounter difficulties.

In both countries, all non-Muslim divorces are handled by the civil courts, while Muslim divorces are handled according to Islamic laws and administered by the respective Syariah Courts. The divorce rate among the Malays is high because of the relative ease of obtaining a divorce. A husband can divorce a wife by simply uttering the word "*talak*" (I divorce you) three times anywhere, in the presence of a witness. On the pronouncement of one or two *talak*s, the divorce is automatic, although the couple can reconcile within 100 days (*iddah*) and the divorce is then revoked (by the man). Divorce is irrevocable when *talak* is pronounced three times. There are other ways in which Muslim divorces may be effected. The first is *fasakh,* in which divorce is granted by the religious judges to the wives in cases of desertion, impotence, failure to maintain a wife or if the man abjures Islam. Under the *cerai taklik,* a divorce may be granted if the groom had contravened the conditions appended to the marriage by the bride's guardian. In *khuluk,* a wife may seek to divorce her husband by offering him a sum of money or some other form of compensation. In Malaysia, men have to apply to the Syariah Court for permission to divorce the wife, although there was a controversy in Malaysia a few years ago over SMS divorce. In 2003, an Islamic court ruled legal a man's action of serving divorce to his wife via a mobile phone text message.[4] The ruling, however, aroused the anger of many women's groups, which feared that women would be taken advantage of in this way. They argued that the divorce should be heard in court so that both sides of the story can be told.

FAMILY AND KINSHIP

Modernization has had an impact on family structure and size, as it has on other aspects of social custom. With increasing educational opportunities and economic progress, many people are getting married later or choosing to remain single. Many married couples are also choosing to have fewer children or no children at all. Like many urbanized and developed countries, Singapore and Malaysia face falling birth rates. In the past two decades, Singapore's birth rate declined by almost 50 percent, from 18 births per 1,000 residents in 1990 to just 9 per 1,000 in 2006.[5] Malaysia's crude birth rate fell from 30 births per 1,000 residents in 1990 to just 21 per 1,000 in 2006.[6] Sociologists have attributed the falling birth rate to the success of policies on population regulation that were introduced to keep population growth in check during the early years of independence. In the immediate postindependence years, both Singapore and Malaysia set up family and population planning agencies to ensure that they would not experience population explosion that could slow the nations' economic development. The Singapore Family Planning and Population Board launched a series of campaigns in 1970s, encouraging Singaporeans to have smaller families. These campaigns promoted slogans such as "Singapore wants small families," "Two-child families in Singapore," and "Boy or girl—two is enough." Together with the legalization of abortion in 1969 in Singapore,[7] such population policies have contributed to the decline in birth rates. But, in recent years, the Singapore government has adopted a "reverse" population policy, this time trying to halt the sliding birth rate by offering couples various economic incentives to have children, such as baby bonuses, various forms of tax relief, and four-month maternity leave.

The Malaysian government introduced a national population control program to reduce the rate of population growth in 1966. This was planned to fit in with the overall economy policy of raising aggregate and per capita income. The program offered family planning services, including the distribution of oral contraceptive pills and intrauterine contraceptive devices through its numerous clinics and health centers across the country. In the mid-1980s, however, there was a sharp u-turn in programs aimed at reducing the country's birth rate. The government adopted a new policy of promoting an increase in the birth rate, with the objective of achieving a population of 70 million by the year 2100. This population policy shift was again tied to the economy; this time, the government wanted to create a larger domestic market to generate and support industrial growth. This policy set off considerable debates about the implications of such an increase for education, housing, health care, and employment, among other issues. The Malaysian government has since adopted several measures in its bid to boost the country's birth rate. The first was the extension of paid maternity leave for female workers in both the public and the private sectors. The second was an increase in the amount of child relief (tax deductions and bonuses). Although the government had announced in 2004 that it was giving up the 70-million target, couples are still being encouraged to have more children.

Despite falling birth rates and decreasing family size, the family remains an important social structure in the Singapore and Malaysian societies. The extended family remains relevant. While they may not all live under the same roof, Singaporeans and Malaysians still interact within the networks of their extended family. These ties are often quite in evidence during festive periods, celebrations, such as birthdays and weddings, and funerals, as relatives are often involved in the preparations of these events. Visiting one's extended families on weekends and public holidays is probably one of the most common leisure activities in Singapore and Malaysia. The nuclear family, with just the parents and children living under the same roof, is now the norm. Except for those who are working interstate (working or living in states other than their home state) or overseas, it is the norm for most children to live with their parents, as is the case in most Asian families. In Singapore, most children do not move out of the family home until they get married and are able to afford a place of their own. Property is expensive, and there is a host of conditions and restrictions—including the need to form a nuclear family of either husband and wife or parent and child—for purchasing government properties, which are usually cheaper than private properties. Thus, many young people cannot afford to live on their own. It is also not unusual for young married couples to stay with one set of parents for some period before they purchase a property of their own.

While modern women are better educated and play an increasingly important role in the economy, especially in comparison to their predecessors, traditional social and religious norms continue to favor the male. The ambitions of the modern women, combined with this traditional perception, have given rise to the problem of the modern superwoman, struggling to cope with work and family. Often, this is seen as a price that women have to pay for wanting to be more than housewives. While there are men who are more open-minded and who participate in housework and childrearing, more often than not, men are much like Homer Simpson, who are more than happy to relegate these duties to the womenfolk. Many families these days hire domestic helpers—usually Filipino, Indonesian, or Sri Lankan girls—to help with the household chores and to care for the young and the elderly in the family. There is an increasing trend of many young children becoming more attached to these servants than their parents, who often work extended hours.

NOTES

1. The percentage of women in the labor force is 54.3 percent for Singapore (2007 figures) and 47.3 percent for Malaysia (2004 figures). Statistics Singapore Web site, http://www.singstat.gov.sg/stats/themes/economy/hist/labour.html, accessed May 12, 2008; Saw Swee Hock, *The Population of Malaysia* (Singapore: Institute of Southeast Asian Studies, 2007), p. 138.

2. *Statistics on Marriages and Divorces 2006* (Singapore: Department of Statistics, 2007), p. 15.

3. *Statistics on Marriages and Divorces 2006* (Singapore: Department of Statistics, 2007). Statistics from Malaysia's Ministry of Women, Family, and Community Development reports: *Muslim marriages by state, 2000–2006; Muslim divorces by state, 2000–2006; Non-Muslim marriages by state, 2000–2006;* and *Non-Muslim divorces by state, 2000–2006.*

4. "Malaysia Permits Text Message Divorce," *BBC News*, July 27, 2003, http://news.bbc.co.uk/2/hi/asia-pacific/3100143.stm, accessed May 15, 2008.

5. *At A Glance: Singapore*, UNICEF Web site, http://www.unicef.org/infobycountry/singapore.html, accessed May 15, 2008.

6. *Malaysia*, UNICEF Web site, http://www.unicef.org/infobycountry/malaysia.html, accessed May 15, 2008.

7. Abortion is still illegal in Malaysia; it is allowed only on medical grounds if the health of the mother is jeopardized. Abortions can still be had at private clinics and maternity homes, but these are often done on the sly without legal authorization.

SUGGESTED READINGS

Djamour, Judith. *Malay Kinship and Marriage in Singapore.* London: Athlone Press, 1965.

Freedman, Maurice. *The Chinese in South-East Asia: A Longer View.* London: China Society, 1965.

Mandakini, Arora. *Small Steps, Giant Leaps: A History of AWARE and the Women's Movement in Singapore.* Singapore: Association of Women for Action and Research, 2007.

Roziah Omar, and Azizah Hamzah (eds.). *Women in Malaysia: Breaking Boundaries.* Kuala Lumpur: Utusan Publications and Distributions, 2003.

Sandhu, K. S., and A. Mani (eds.). *Indian Communities in Southeast Asia.* Singapore: Institute of Southeast Asian Studies, 2006.

8

Festivals and Leisure Activities

THE FESTIVE CALENDARS of Singapore and Malaysia are tightly packed, with a festival happening at least once every other month. All the ethnic groups have their own festivals, adding to the color and excitement in multicultural Singapore and Malaysia. In recent years, traditional festivals have been joined by more modern ones, which are less ethnically based. They have emerged as a result of nation-building, and some are highly influenced by tourism.

TRADITIONAL FESTIVALS

Many of the traditional festivals in Singapore and Malaysia are ethnically based, and many have religious origins. These festivals are linked to lunar calendars—which track time through the movement of the moon—rather than the modern Gregorian calendar. As a result, there are no fixed dates for the festivals; their dates change from year to year.

Malay/Indigenous

Hari Raya Aidilfitri and Hari Raya Haji

The Malays share their festive calendar with many Muslims across the world, though many customs have been localized. However, there are only two visibly significant Malay festivals in Singapore and Malaysia. More commonly known as Hari Raya Puasa in Singapore and Malaysia, Hari Raya Aidilfitri is a major Muslim festival. It is a celebration of the end of Ramadan, the

Muslim month of fasting, and it falls on the first day of the 10th lunar month of the Islamic calendar. The end of Ramadan is marked by the sighting of the new moon in the month of Shawal. A busy period of preparation precedes the celebration. Muslim families busy themselves with cleaning the house, purchasing new household items and clothing, baking cakes and sweets, and cooking delicacies in anticipation of the celebrations. The purchasing of new items is a symbol of a renewal and celebration, which is part and parcel of the local culture. The festivities are marked by the phenomenon of *balik kampung,* which literally means going back to the village. In the week leading up to the festivities, many Muslims who work outside their hometowns return for the celebrations. This is especially marked in Malaysia, where many people work and study in major cities and towns in various states, including Singapore.

On the morning of Hari Raya Puasa, children greet their parents and ask for forgiveness and blessings. This is followed by a visit to the mosque and the graves of deceased family members after breakfast. On this day, children receive gifts, usually a token sum of money wrapped in a green envelope. During the festivities, it is also customary for friends and families to visit one another, exchange good wishes, and partake of cakes, cookies, and other delicacies prepared for the occasion. Although the festivities usually last for a month, in highly urbanized Singapore and Malaysia, most of the activities take place in the first three days. But many Muslims continue to celebrate with visits throughout the month.

The other celebration on the Islamic calendar is Hari Raya Haji (also known as Hari Raya aidil Adha, the Festival of Sacrifice), which follows approximately two months after Hari Raya Puasa. The Haji celebrations are simpler in Singapore and Malaysia than in Saudi Arabia, and are less elaborate than those for Hari Raya Puasa. The reason is that Hari Raya Haji is celebrated only by those who have performed the *haj,* the pilgrimage to the holy city of Mecca. To mark the end of the pilgrimage and to commemorate Prophet Muhammad's willingness to sacrifice his son, many mosques and Muslim institutions perform the sacrificial slaughtering of goats and cattle. The meat is then distributed to people in the neighborhood, especially the needy and the poor.

Harvest Festivals

Given their simple lifestyle, the indigenous tribes in Malaysia do not have many major festive celebrations except for the harvest festival and those that commemorate rites of passage. Among these celebrations of the various indigenous tribes in Sabah and Sarawak, the harvest festivals are most significant. Although known by different names and with variations in customs, these festivals are a time to give thanks for the harvest and offer prayers for future bounties. In Sabah, the Tadau Ka'amantan (Harvest Festival) is the most significant festival of its largest ethnic group, the Kadazans. The festival honors the Bambaazon, the spirit of the *padi* (rice) plant, which features significantly in the life and culture of the agricultural Kadazans. During the festival, the *bobohizan* (high priestess) performs an elaborate ritual of chanting and prayers to thank, restore, and feed the Bambaazon.

In Sarawak, the harvest festival is known as Gawai Dayak. Like Sabah's Tadau Ka'amantan, the Gawai Dayak is held at the end of harvest. The main feature of the Gawai Dayak is the *miring,* the ceremonial offering of food and *tuak* (rice wine) to the gods. In preparation, members of the Dayak community clean their homes thoroughly and also their ancestors' graves. On the eve of the festival, the youngest family member offers a specially prepared dish to their parents to symbolize respect. The oldest family member makes a speech giving advice to the family. At midnight, all members of the longhouse gather as the chief performs the *sampi* ritual to pray for longevity.

Since the 1960s, the respective state governments have fixed the date of these festivals and declared them public holidays. In Sabah, the Tadau Ka'amantan was fixed on the last two days of May, while Sarawak's *Gawai Dayak* is set between May 31 and June 1. Such festivals have also become

Tuak (rice wine) is a staple drink for Sarawak's indigenous peoples. Courtesy of the author.

increasingly nonexclusive. The performances of traditional dances during the festivals, for example, have been brought out of the communities into public places such as hotels and shopping complexes. In Sarawak, the festival is celebrated with a special parade, the *ngiring kenyalang,* in which the different ethnic groups dress in their traditional costumes and march in a parade.

Chinese

The Chinese place a strong emphasis on familial ties and respect for the elders and ancestors, which is reflected in many of the Chinese festivals celebrated in Singapore and Malaysia. Most of these festivals originated in Chinese culture's rich reserve of folk beliefs and in the traditional agricultural society. Although the Chinese seem to celebrate more festivals than the other ethnic groups, the younger generation is selective and observes only the more significant ones. This is especially so as many Chinese have converted to Christianity—Buddhism, Taoism, and folk religion being the religious norm—and thus have less interest in festivals based on folk belief and superstition. The younger generation is also less interested in continuing with these traditional customs, which are sometimes seen as old-fashioned and superstitious.

Chinese New Year

The Chinese New Year (CNY) is the most widely celebrated festival of Chinese communities all over the world. The CNY falls on the first day of the first lunar month (usually January or February). Each year is named after and hosted by one of the 12 Chinese zodiac animals—rat, ox, tiger, rabbit, dragon, snake, horse, sheep, monkey, chicken, dog, and pig. As it signifies the beginning of the year, the CNY is often preceded by a period of spring cleaning. Many families also decorate their houses with auspicious motifs, usually in red, considered the luckiest color. Crowds throng Chinatowns in Singapore and Malaysia to do their festive shopping and to stock up on foodstuff, sweets, and other treats. One of the most important customs is the reunion dinner on the eve of the CNY. This is an occasion where all the members of the family, who may not usually have the chance to eat together, gather for a sumptuous feast. Family members who live overseas often come home especially for this dinner. After dinner, many maintain a night vigil to welcome the CNY at midnight. The Chinese believe that the final hours of the evening mark the return of the Kitchen God from his annual pilgrimage to the Heavens. These days, special variety programs are broadcast over television throughout the evening. Many also head to the temples to offer the first prayers for the new year or to Chinatown to do some last-minute shopping.

Many Singaporeans flock to Chinatown to do their Chinese New Year shopping.
Courtesy of the author.

The CNY is a time when folk beliefs are at their most prominent, many
of them manifested through customs. Take, for example, the exchanging of
oranges during the festivities. Phonetically, the word for mandarin oranges
sounds like the word for gold in the Cantonese dialect; oranges are thus symbols of good luck. The oranges must always be given in pairs, as even numbers
are considered more auspicious than odd numbers. The even-number superstition is extended to the tradition of the giving of *ang pows* (red packets).
It is customary for senior and married family members to give red packets
containing money to the younger and single members of the family as a token
of good luck. The amount given in the red packet must be in even numbers.
Sweeping is generally forbidden during the first few days of the festivities as
many believe that sweeping the floor during this period means sweeping away
the good luck.

Traditionally, the New Year's celebrations are to last for 15 days. In Singapore and Malaysia, however, the most important activities, such as visiting
relatives and friends, are done in the first few days. There are two other
significant days within the CNY period. The first is Ren Ri (man's birthday),
on the seventh day of the CNY, which is typically celebrated with the consumption of a raw fish salad known as *yu sheng*. A tradition created by several
Singaporean chefs, the salad is mixed together by tossing it in the air (*lou hei*)
with chopsticks while reciting good wishes for the new year. The second is

Chap Goh Meh, which falls on the 15th day and marks the end of CNY. This day is the Chinese Valentine's Day, traditionally a night of courtship and matchmaking. In Singapore, CNY has also become a major tourist festival with two nationwide celebrations: River Hong Bao and the Chingay Parade. River Hong Bao is an annual fete showcasing Chinese cultural performances, traditional art, and foodstuff. The Chingay Parade is a street parade, held during the first weekend of the CNY, that features elaborate floats, songs, and dances. When the Chingay Parade was first introduced, in 1973, it featured only traditional acts such as stilt-walking and martial arts by locals. Since then, the parade has expanded to include overseas performers and nontraditional performances.

Qing Ming

In April, many Chinese Singaporeans and Malaysians visit the graves of their departed relatives to pay their respects on Qing Ming. Literally meaning "clear and bright," Qing Ming is similar to All Souls' Day. It is customary on this day to tend to the graves of one's ancestors and to offer food, drinks, and incense to the deceased. Offerings of paper money and worldly goods such as radios and television sets made of papier mâché are burned. In Singapore, burial is now not as common as it used to be. Given the lack of land, cremation has replaced burial as a more practical and convenient way of disposing the dead. Many Chinese families continue to observe Qing Ming rituals at the columbarium (a place where urns containing ashes of the dead are housed).

Vesak

Vesak Day, or Wesak, as it is also known in Malaysia, is one of the grandest Buddhist festivals in Singapore and Malaysia. It falls in the third Chinese lunar month and the sixth lunar month on the Hindu calendar (usually April/May). Vesak Day commemorates the birth, enlightenment, and final passing away (*parinnibbana*) of the Buddha. On this day, devotees pray and chant in the temple and offer alms to monks, and the day is commemorated by myriad processional and temple activities, including open-air blessings of devotees by monks.

Dragon Boat Festival

The Dragon Boat Festival originated as a day to commemorate Qu Yuan (c. 340–278 B.C.), a court minister during the Chinese Warring States period (475–221 B.C.) who committed suicide by jumping into a river as protest against the corrupt practices of the court. In a bid to save Qu Yuan's body

On Qing Ming, it is customary to tend to the graves of the ancestors and offer food, drinks, and incense. Courtesy of the author.

from being eaten by the fish, his friends rowed boats into the river and beat the water with oars to scare the fish away. They also threw rice dumplings (*zong zi* in Mandarin) into the river as bait for the fish. This legend gave rise to two customs that are still practiced today: the eating of rice dumplings and the dragon boat races. The dumplings are made from glutinous rice filled with a combination of meat, dates, egg yolk, beans, chestnuts, and mushrooms and wrapped in banana leaves before being steamed. There are also plain dumplings that can be eaten with sugar. Some families maintain the tradition of wrapping their own dumplings, although this tradition is fast fading, as it is much more convenient to buy ready-made ones at stalls and supermarkets.

The most exciting part of the festival is the dragon boat races. Dragon boats are brightly painted fiberglass boats, spanning 40 to 100 feet in length, the form of a dragon, an auspicious creature in Chinese mythology. The boat is powered by as many as 80 rowers, with a drummer and a flag catcher leading at the bow with rhythmic drumming. Dragon boat competitions now attract the participation of international teams and are spectacular events for tourists and locals alike. Today, dragon boat races are no longer confined just to this festive season. Since 1989, dragon boat races have become part of the Southeast Asian Games.

Hungry Ghost Festival

One of the most colorful Chinese festivals is the Hungry Ghost Festival, observed by Chinese communities during the seventh lunar month. Taoists believe that the gates of hell are flung open during this month (usually August or September), and spirits are allowed to roam the earth. Unlike Qing Ming, the Hungry Ghost Festival is a festival for the condemned souls in hell who have no relief from their suffering. A common sight during the festival is the burning of incense and joss papers. It is believed that these offerings to the "hungry ghosts" will prevent them from causing harm to oneself and family. Superstitious families also avoid organizing major activities such as weddings during this "unlucky" period. In addition, communities often stage performances such as Chinese opera or, in more recent times, the *ge tai* (street variety shows) to entertain the ghosts. An auction and dinner known as Zhong Yuan Hui is also held in conjunction with these activities. During the dinner, items such as electronic goods, daily necessities and symbolic items such as charcoal (known as "black gold") are offered for auction. The proceeds from the auction go towards paying for the following year's dinner and auction.

Mid-Autumn Festival

Unlike the Hungry Ghost Festival, the Mid-Autumn festival is a joyous occasion. Commonly known as the Mooncake Festival, it falls on the 15th day of the lunar eighth month (around September) and is a homage to the moon goddess, Chang Er. According to Chinese mythology, Chang Er was the wife of an archer, Hou Yi, who successfully shot down 9 of the 10 suns scorching the earth. As a reward for this deed, he was chosen by the Chinese people as their king. Unfortunately, he was a tyrannical ruler, and, to make matters worse, he stole the elixir of life in a bid to live forever. To save the people from his tyranny, Chang Er swallowed the elixir of life and found herself floating to the moon, where she is believed to have remained to the present day. The moon is believed to be at its roundest and brightest on the day this festival is celebrated, and legend has it that one can see Chang Er in the moon if one looks closely.

On the evening of the festival, children and adults gather at the open spaces of their housing estates or in their gardens to eat mooncakes and to drink tea and *shang yue* (look at the moon). There is a wide variety of mooncakes, a type of Chinese pastry eaten only during the festival. Traditional mooncakes are filled with red bean paste or lotus seed paste, while more modern unbaked "snow-skinned" mooncakes are made from glutinous rice flour and sugar. New mooncake flavors are also constantly introduced—ice-cream, mango, and cream cheese, just to name a few. As the adults eat mooncakes and sip endless cups of tea, the children parade around their garden or park with colorful lanterns. Lanterns vary in shape and size. They range from those made of colored cellophane papers and bamboo strips to lanterns depicting cartoon characters and battery-operated plastic lanterns that have blinking lights and play children's jingles.

Winter Solstice

Winter Solstice is usually the last festival of the year for the Chinese community and normally falls between December 21 and 23. It marks the beginning of winter, and, according to Chinese beliefs, it is the time when the Earth God returns to the Heavens to report on the goings-on in the world. Even though there is no winter in Singapore and Malaysia, the local Chinese community continues to observe this festival as an opportunity for family reunion. On this day, most Chinese families have dinner together and eat a special desert of *tang yuan*—glutinous rice balls boiled in a sweet soup. This homemade variety is plain, but those purchased in supermarkets come with a variety of fillings, including red bean paste and peanut paste, two of the most popular.

Indian

The Indian community in Singapore and Malaysia draw on a rich Hindu culture. The Indian communities in Singapore comprise various groups such as the Tamils, Punjabis, Gujuratis, Bengalis, and Sindhis, among others. Although there are several festivals celebrated by Hindus all over the world, mostly harvest festivals, the two most celebrated Indian festivals in Singapore and Malaysia are Thaipusam and Deepavali.

Thaipusam

Thaipusam commemorates the day Lord Murugan (also known as Subramanium) was presented with a golden spear (the Nyana Vel) to fight the evil Soorapadman. As one of the most important religious festivals of the Hindus, Thaipusam is a day of prayer and thanksgiving. Devotees prepare themselves for this day through fasting and prayers. The most spectacular display of a Hindu's devotion on this day is the carrying of *kavadis* (burdens) as a fulfillment of their vows to Lord Murugan. The *kavadi* associated with Thaipusam is the *vel kavadi*, a huge *kavadi* made of skewers and spears, which devotees carry by attaching it to their bodies, cheeks, and tongues. Carrying the *vel kavadi* is not compulsory, and devotees, especially women, carry simpler *kavadi*s such as *paal kavadi* (a pot of fresh milk), *pushpa* (flowers), *kerembu* (sugarcane), *elani* (young coconut), and *mayil* (peacock feathers) *kavadi*s.

In Singapore, on the morning of Thaipusam, a procession of devotees carrying their various *kavadis* travel on foot from the main thoroughfare of Little India to one of the main Hindu temples in Singapore. In Malaysia, the largest celebration takes place in the Batu Caves at the outskirts of Kuala Lumpur. The Batu Caves, which house one of the largest temples in Malaysia to Lord Murugan, is one of the holiest sites for Hindus in Malaysia. On the eve of Thaipusam each year, a 5-ton silver chariot bearing Lord Murugan's image embarks on an 8-hour, 9.3-mile procession from the Sri Mahamariamman Temple in Kuala Lumpur to the Batu Caves. Until 2000, the chariot was pulled by six bulls. The bulls have since been replaced by a motorized vehicle.

Deepavali

Deepavali, or the Festival of Lights, usually falls between October and November. It is a highly symbolic day for the Hindus. Also known as Diwali, Deepavali is often mistaken for a celebration of the Indian new year. Deepavali celebrates not the new year but rather a new beginning—the triumph of light over dark, of good over evil. In Hindu mythology, it is the day Lord Krishna defeated the evil demon, Narakasura.

There are many rituals associated with Deepavali. Devotees take oil baths, which symbolize purification and a new beginning, visit the temple, and break coconuts. The hard shell of the coconut represents egos and pride, which must be broken in order to achieve humility and purity, symbolized by the white flesh of the fruit. On this day, oil lamps are also lit in the house as it is believed that the light from the lamps acts as a guide for the wondering souls of the departed. This tradition probably originated in one of the many Hindu mythologies associated with Deepavali in which Lord Rama returned to Ayodhya after a 14-year exile and a battle in which he killed the demon king, Ravana. It is believed that the people of Ayodhya lit oil lamps along the way to light his path in the darkness.

It is also customary for many Hindus in Singapore and Malaysia to decorate the entrances to their homes with a *kolam* for the festival. The *kolam* is an intricate floor drawing colored with different hues of dyed flour that is meant to invoke the blessings of Lakshimi, the Goddess of Wealth. One of the main features of the *kolam* is symmetry, which represents the idea of universal balance, one of the key values of Hindu beliefs. In Singapore and Malaysia, a popular *kolam* symbol is the *sahasradala padmam,* a thousand-petal lotus that is the symbol of purity.

Eurasian/Christian

Since the arrival of the Europeans in Southeast Asia, Christianity has become a growing religion among the local population. Most Eurasians are

Christian, and their festivals are inspired by the Christian tradition. However, many Chinese and some people of most ethnic groups (with the exception of the Malays, who are almost universally Muslim) are also Christians and participate in Easter and Christmas commemorations, as well.

Festa San Pedro

For about a week in June, the relatively small Portuguese Eurasian community in Malacca celebrates the Feast of St. Peter with great fanfare. The carnival, usually held during the last week of June, honors the patron of the fishermen, St. Peter. This festival is rooted in the heritage of the community, many of whom were fishermen or were involved in some way with the fishing industry in the early years. The Portuguese Eurasian community of Malacca has been celebrating the festival since the 1930s, when their community was established. The festival is a colorful celebration of games, cultural performances, and food fairs. There are also blessings for fishing boats, part of the heritage of Malacca and the early Portuguese. Fishing boats are festooned with banners, lights, and historical relics reminiscent of the 16th-century Portuguese era, and there is a competition for the best-decorated boat.

Good Friday and Easter Sunday

Good Friday and Easter Sunday are important dates commemorated in churches all around Singapore and Malaysia. These commemorations take the form of re-enactments of the final days, crucifixion, and resurrection of Christ, and midnight vigils are held during special church services. These special days still maintain their religious tone, unlike in many Western countries, where Easter has come to mean chocolate bunnies and Easter egg hunts.

Christmas

Christmas is one of the most celebrated festive seasons in Singapore and Malaysia. With the rapid modernization of the two societies, the celebration of Christmas has extended beyond Christian groups to the general masses and has taken on more commercial overtones. While Christians commemorate Christmas at church services and performances, non-Christians join them in Christmas shopping and feasting. Shopping centers in both Singapore and Malaysia are often specially decorated in anticipation of the festive season. Even fast-food restaurants are decked out in Christmas decorations. Restaurants and cafés often offer Christmas menus, including roast turkey and ham. Among the most popular item for the season is the Christmas log cake, which can be bought at most major bakeries and restaurants. Since 1984, the Singapore Tourism Board has organized the annual Christmas Light-Up and a contest for the best-decorated building in the country's prime shopping area along Orchard Road. Between November and January each year, the whole shopping stretch is lit up by millions of lights that adorn the trees and lampposts on both sides of the road. Elaborate decorations often front the façades of the numerous shopping malls, one of which is chosen as the best-decorated building. Often, such decorations incorporate Chinese New Year or Hari Raya motifs and figures, especially when the festivals occur within a month of one another.

If not for the warm weather, one would think one was in a large American city with the festive lights, Christmas trees, carolers, shopping-center Santas, and frenzied buying going on. Families and friends also take the opportunity to gather for Christmas parties, often with traditional Christmas food (which is foreign to local palates), such as roast turkey, ham, and Christmas log cake,

Since 1984, the Singapore Tourism Board has organized the annual Christmas Light-Up and a contest for the best-decorated building in the country's prime shopping area along Orchard Road during the Christmas season. Courtesy of the author.

usually purchased from supermarkets or upmarket Western eateries. Rather than a religious occasion, Christmas has become more and more a secular celebration to mark the end of the year.

NEW FESTIVALS

"New" festivals are those without an ethnic or cultural origin. Instead, these festivals are often instituted celebrations that have developed in the past three decades and are largely celebrated by Singaporeans and Malaysians of all races and religions. A number of these festivals have also been developed as cultural attractions for tourism, an important pillar of the Singapore and Malaysian economies.

Independence or National Day

Singapore and Malaysia celebrate their independence on August 9 and August 31, respectively, each year. Since 1965, Singapore has celebrated its independence—freedom from British and Malaysian rule—with a grand parade. The National Day Parade (NDP) is a spectacular performance put on by the armed forces, schools, and various community groups that has become bigger and grander each year. Because of the highly choreographed nature of the parade, preparations and rehearsals begin about a year in advance of the event. Although the NDP is broadcast over television and streamed on the Internet, tickets to the actual event are in such high demand that they are distributed through a national ballot. Highlights of the parade include fly-bys executed by the air force's fighter jets, performances of specially written songs by local pop stars, elaborate mass dances, and, of course, the most impressive fireworks of the year. Malaysia also celebrates its national day, known as Merdeka Day (Independence Day), to commemorate Malaysia's independence from the British, in 1957. Until 2003, the celebrations were hosted in the capital, Kuala Lumpur. Since then, the celebrations have been moved to Putrajaya, the country's new administrative district, located 15.5 mile south of the capital.

While the circumstances of their independence are different, there are several similarities between the national day parades of Singapore and Malaysia. Like Singapore's National Day celebrations, Malaysia's parades are based on a theme that helps forge the national identity and mirrors the stage of the country's development. For example, in the early 1970s, when Malaysia had just embarked on development, national day themes include "Love and Unity" (1971), "Progressive Society" (1972), "Fair Society" (1973), and "A Society with Malaysian Culture" (1974). Dignitaries are always present for the *merdeka* parade, which includes the singing of the national anthem and recitation of the national oath, marching military and community groups, floats, and aerial displays. Usually, for a month before and after the National Day, national flags deck the residential houses and public buildings of both countries as a sign of patriotism. In Singapore and Malaysia, the national flag is normally not displayed publicly, except in schools and government buildings.

Arts and Cultural Festivals

In the past decade or so, new festivals have been added to showcase local contemporary and traditional cultures. Singapore's cultural calendar features two arts-related festivals. The first is the annual Singapore Arts Festival, which was started in 1977 as a national arts festival featuring local performances and exhibitions. The festival has since expanded to include international artists and several hundred activities spread out over a month. The second major arts-related festival is the annual Singapore International Film Festival (SIFF). Launched in 1987 in an effort to highlight independent and noncommercial films, the SIFF has become the platform where many Southeast Asian filmmakers premier their works. Many local filmmakers also started their careers by participating in the Festival.

Malaysia's arts calendar is also packed. In the past few years, Malaysia has launched several national arts festivals to showcase its vibrant arts scene. In 2006, it launched the Kuala Lumpur Festival as a platform for local arts and cultural communities. Although local arts are the main attraction, the festival also features international acts, such as the All American Boys Choir. Malaysian-made films compete in the annual Malaysian Film Festival, held since 1980, and winners are chosen in five categories: Best Feature Film, Best Digital Film, Best Animation, Best Short Film, and Best Documentary. In 2007, another film festival, the Kuala Lumpur International Film Festival, was launched. Unlike the Malaysian Film Festival, the KLIFF has a more international approach, screening films from all over the world.

There are several tourism- and leisure-related events throughout the year in Singapore and Malaysia. Malaysia, for example, hosts the annual nationwide Colors of Malaysia (Warna-Warna Malaysia) in the middle of the year. Organized by the Tourism Ministry, it is a showcase of the different cuisines, arts, and cultures of the various states. Promotions by hotels, cultural shows, and extravaganzas are also common. Singapore and Malaysia capitalize on the shopping and eating theme to attract tourists. While Singapore has The Great Singapore Sale in June, the two major sales in Malaysia are the Mega Malaysia Sale Carnival (midyear) and the Malaysia Year End Sale (year end). During these sales, many retailers, from those in shopping malls to those with individual stalls on the street, sell their products, from jewelry and fashion wear to consumer electronics, at heavily discounted prices. Promotions such as the Great Singapore Shopping Challenge, in which shoppers compete to be the "ultimate bargain-hunter," further enhance the popularity of these events.

Food has also been a tourist draw. In Singapore, an annual Food Festival is organized by the Singapore Tourism Board as a showcase for the wide variety of local cuisines. Activities conducted during the festival include culinary classes and workshops, cooking demonstrations, food carnivals, and promotions at the various eating outlets. The Malaysia International Gourmet Festival, launched in 2001, is an annual food feast that aims to promote the fine-dining culture in Malaysia. During the festival, the participating restaurants offer special deals and menus by their renowned chefs. Events such as cooking classes and gourmet tours are also organized. One of the most anticipated events of the festival is the awards ceremony, at which prizes are given to participating restaurants and chefs for their achievements.

LEISURE ACTIVITIES

Traditionally, the pastimes of Singaporeans and Malaysians have been simple. Children played games using whatever materials were available in their natural environment. Popular games for girls included hopscotch and "five-stones." While hopscotch is a favorite all over the world, "five-stones" is variation of "jacks" as played in America. Instead of using a ball and "jacks," the locals make their own "stones" by filling small triangular cloth sacs with rice, beans, or sago seeds. These "stones" are then thrown and caught in a specific sequence. Another game favored by the girls is "zero-point" or the "rubber band game." The main "tool" of the game is a rope made out of several hundred rubber bands tied to one another. Two players hold the ends of the rope taut while the other players take turns jumping over the rope without touching it. Players may touch the rope when the game has progressed to a certain point.

Among the boys, *chaptek* used to be a favorite. *Chaptek* is a small shuttlecock-like item that is made from chicken feathers nailed to two pieces of rubber. The aim of the game is to keep the *chaptek* in the air for as long as possible by a series of well-placed kicks. The game can be played individually or in groups. *Congkak* is a traditional game favored by Malay children. It is a game for two, played using a wooden board with 14 holes arranged in sets of 7 on the edges of the board and some seeds or glass marbles. The objective of the game is to gather as many *congkak* seeds into the player's "storehouse," which is located on one side of the board. This is done by "sowing," a process in which a player gathers up the seeds in any one of the holes and places one seed in each hole, except for the opponent's "storehouse." If the last seed falls into an empty hole, the opponent gets his turn to play. But if the last seed falls into the player's own "storehouse," he gets another turn. The game continues until a player either has no more seeds in his houses (the holes on his side of the board and the storehouse) or concedes defeat.

Many young Singaporeans and Malaysians these days have traded these traditional games for more modern computer games. It is common to find children and young adults alike playing with their portable gaming consoles in most cities of Malaysia and Singapore. Many of the younger generation are also adept at role-playing games, usually played on networked computers. Singapore has sent teams to take part in various international cybergame tournaments and has won the gold medal in the 2008 World Cyber Games, the equivalent of the Olympics in the gaming world. In 2005, Singapore hosted the grand finals of the World Cyber Games. Malaysia is also an active participant in the World Cyber Games, ranking 27th in the world in 2008. There are numerous Internet cafés around the cities of Malaysia and Singapore that have a section dedicated to computer games.

Even as new technology is winning popularity, Malaysia especially has sought to preserve some of these traditional games, considered part of the Malay culture. Two of these, kite flying and top spinning, are kept alive by large-scale festivals. Every June, Kelantan, a northeastern Malaysian state considered the heart of Malay culture, hosts a five-day festival known as Pesta Wau (Festival of Kites) to celebrate the age-old tradition of kite flying, a favorite pastime during the postharvest season. One of the earliest mentions of kite flying can be found in the *Sejarah Melayu*. Kelantan is famous for its kites. Kelantanese kites are ornately designed, with elaborate motifs made from cut-out paper designs. They typically measure about 3 to 4 feet in length. Large kites can stretch up to 20 feet from wingtip to wingtip. Traditionally handcrafted from bamboo strips, paper, acetate, and string, these kites are becoming increasingly rare because there are fewer young people learning these traditional skills. The Pesta Wau has developed from a local community harvest celebration into one that attracts tourists and international participants from across Malaysia, Singapore, China, Europe, and even the United States. The kite-flying competition is scored on the kite's design, the flight angle (the more vertical, the higher the score), airborne stability, and the music of the kite (a melodious and droning note that the bow fastened to the kite's neck generates when the kite is airborne).

Kelantan also hosts an annual top-spinning tournament. Tops, or *gasing*, as it is locally known, is a traditional Malay game. The *gasing* comes in various shapes and sizes. Plate-shaped, heart-shaped, flat-top, and egg-shaped *gasings* are native to the region and come in sizes as small as a golf ball or as large as a human head. The *gasing* is usually made of wood, iron, lead, and sometimes even firm fruits such as the guava. A string is wound tightly around the *gasing,* and, when it is released, it sets the top spinning. There are two main kinds of top competitions: a spinning contest and a striking contest. In the spinning contest, the objective is to keep the top spinning for as long as possible, whereas in a striking match, the objective is to strike at an opposing top to try to topple it. The tournament in Kelantan's *gasing* festival is a spinning contest in which many teams across Malaysia participate. One of the records set was a top that spun for about two hours.

Sports

Some traditional sports are still being played. *Sepak takraw* is a game that has been played for several hundred years in Malaysia. With a name that literally means "kick ball," the game uses a small woven rattan ball and is played like volleyball, except that hands are not used. Instead, players handle the ball with the feet, knee, chest, and head. Players are divided into two teams of three each, and the game is played on a court about the size of a badminton court. *Sepak takraw* is now an official game in the Southeast Asia Games (SEA Games) and the Asian Games.

Another traditional sport that still has a large following in Singapore and Malaysia is the traditional Malay martial art form, *silat.* Also known as *pencak silat,* the martial art form can also be performed as traditional dance. Like many forms of traditional martial arts, *silat* is often regarded as an art of self-defense rather than of combat. Today, *silat* is an official sport in the SEA Games. There are also many practitioners of *qigong,* a component of Chinese martial art that utilizes the movement and circulation of breath in the body. Also closely related to the Buddhist and Taoist practice of meditation, *qigong* has numerous variations. Today, many regard *qigong* as a form of healthy exercise. One can often see groups practicing *qigong* in the parks and public spaces in housing estates.

In Singapore and Malaysia, modern sporting games have active followings. Football, or soccer, is a passion shared by both Singaporeans and Malaysians and is considered the national sport. In the 1970s, the most anticipated sporting event of the year was the annual Malaysian Cup competition in which the constant rivalry between the two nations was played out on the field, attracting huge crowds on both sides. This friendly soccer rivalry faded when Singapore withdrew from the Malaysia Cup in 1995 to set up its own league, known as the S-League (Singapore League). Despite local teams' lack of international success, soccer continues to be one of the most popular sports played in schools and amateur clubs, as well as the most watched sport on television.

The English Premier League is one of the most avidly followed soccer leagues in both countries.

Another popular sport is badminton. Malaysia ranks among the world's top badminton countries. With its roots in an old English children's game, badminton was probably brought to Malaysia by British colonial officers. The annual Malaysia Open badminton tournament has been held in Malaysia since 1937, with two stoppages: one during the Second World War between 1942 and 1946 and the other from 1967 to 1982. Singapore also has a keen badminton-playing populace. Various clubs and school competitions are held annually across the country. Golf is another popular sport in Singapore and Malaysia that was introduced by the British more than a century ago. Once a sport for the rich, golf is today becoming more commonly accepted, although it is still not a game for the masses. Despite the countries' small size, there are about 15 golf courses in Singapore and more than 200 across Malaysia, attesting to the popularity of the game. Many Singaporeans and Malaysians are avid swimmers, given the region's year-round summer weather. Hockey, street soccer, inline-skating, basketball, and cycling are also among the more popular sporting activities of the young.

Singaporeans and Malaysians are enthusiastic motorsport enthusiasts. Grand Prix races were held at various locations in Singapore and Malaysia in the 1960s and 1970s. As the races in Singapore cut back, Malaysia continued to host several racing tournaments, including the international Formula Two and Formula Holden races. Since 1999, Malaysia has hosted the Formula One (F1) races at the Sepang International Circuit at Sepang, which was built for this event. Besides the annual F1 races, the Sepang circuit also hosts kart-racing and motocross tournaments. In 2008, Singapore hosted the first night race in F1 history. The race was conducted in the heart of Singapore's colonial and business district and was the F1's first street circuit in Asia. A purpose-built circuit for this annual race will be completed in 2010.

In recent years, there have been concerted efforts by the Singapore government to develop its sporting capabilities. In 2008, the city successfully won the bid to host the inaugural Youth Olympic Games in 2010. Since the 1950s, Singapore athletes have not had much success in the international arena. During the 2008 Olympics, the Singapore women's table-tennis team won a silver medal, breaking what has been termed a medal drought in the sporting community. But the win was followed by controversy; all the members of the women's table-tennis team were China-born individuals who had been given Singapore citizenship under the government's Foreign Talent Sports policy. The policy was introduced in the 1990s to boost Singapore's competitiveness in the international sports scene. But many Singaporeans questioned the appropriateness of importing foreign talents to represent

Singapore. But, with Singaporeans more concerned with academic success than with sporting success, many parents are reluctant to let their children develop a career in sports. As part of the effort to provide a more conducive environment for young athletes, the Singapore government established a sports school in 2004 where aspiring athletes can focus on training in their chosen field without sacrificing their studies.

In 1988, sports was elevated to a national issue in Malaysia. The impetus was the Malaysian public's dismay at the athletes' lack of success in the international sporting arena. Malaysia has participated in the Olympics since 1956 but has not won any medals. In 1988, the Malaysian government adopted a National Sports Policy, with the aim of developing the country's sporting facilities and training capabilities. Funding was provided for the building of sporting venues, and incentives were given to boost athletes' performances. Malaysia has since won several Olympic medals in the 1992, 1996, and 2008 Olympics in badminton. The medals in the 1992 and 1996 Olympics were won by the Sidek brothers—Abdul Rashid Mohamed Sidek, Razif Sidek, and Jalani Sidek—who dominated the international badminton scene during the 1990s. Lee Chong Wei, one of the world's top badminton players, won a silver medal in the 2008 Olympics. For his achievement, Lee was given the title of "Datuk," the Malaysian equivalent of a British knighthood.

SUGGESTED READINGS

Achievements Off the Beaten Track: Stories of Singapore Sports Veterans. Singapore: Candid Creation, 2005.

De Cotta, Ian. *The Singapore Grand Prix: 50 Years in the Making.* Singapore: MediaCorp.

Leong, Gregory. *Festivals of Malaysia.* Selangor: Pelanduk Publications, 1992.

Pham, Duc Thanh (ed.). *Traditional Festivals of ASEAN.* Hanoi: ASEAN Committee on Culture and Information, 2003.

Through the Decades: Malaysia's 50 Years of Sporting Glory. Selangor: E Publication in association with SEN Media, 2007.

9

The Future of Singapore and Malaysian Culture

MODERNIZATION AND GLOBALIZATION are significantly transforming culture and customs in Singapore and Malaysia. Although these have been discussed briefly in earlier chapters, this chapter explores in detail some of these changes and the directions in which Singapore/Malaysian culture are heading. These include the growth of Singlish and Manglish, local versions of spoken English in Singapore and Malaysia, which are regarded variously as a source of solidarity and national pride and as a wellspring of local humor. At the same time, many regard these new languages as a source of embarrassment that needs to be corrected. Another topic we touch on is multiculturalism, a distinctive feature of Singapore and Malaysian societies as a result of large-scale immigration, especially in the 19th century. Seen as a whole, the various groups enrich the cultural resources of the countries, resulting in vibrant and diverse festivals, cuisine, fashion, and architecture. On the other hand, ethnic and religious differences have historically been, and continue to be, a constant source of internal tension, which the respective governments manage in their own ways. On top of interethnic tensions, Singaporeans and Malaysians struggle to balance the pull of tradition, which roots their cultural identities, and the lure of modernity and globalization. Both Singapore and Malaysia have invested heavily in information technology and new media. These moves toward a modern and global identity have had a major effect on traditional culture and customs.

Although Singapore and Malaysia share many cultural similarities—as we have seen in the previous chapters—the two countries and their people are also different in significant ways. Despite being tied by geography, history, and economy, the countries have a relationship that is far from harmonious. While frequently cooperative, Singaporeans and Malaysians are also competitive and often hold negative attitudes toward each other. On the political level, the two governments are also in a love-hate relationship, at times harmonious, at times antagonistic. Nevertheless, interactions between the two countries are inevitable, and, despite the political differences, the shared culture and customs form a solid basis for developing better understanding between the two countries.

SINGAPORE/MALAYSIAN ENGLISH

One of the legacies of British colonization has been the introduction of the English language and English education into the region. Increasingly, Singaporeans and Malaysians speak English as if it were their first language. Especially in Singapore, English is the language of business and government and serves as a medium for interethnic communication. It is often easier to recognize Singaporeans or Malaysians by the way they speak than by the way they look. Local versions of English have become a distinct cultural marker. The local colloquial versions of English are known unflatteringly as Singlish (Singapore English) and Manglish (Malaysian English). These versions differ strongly from standard English and borrow heavily from Chinese dialects, Malay, Tamil, and other native languages, leaving non-Singaporean and non-Malaysian English speakers scratching their heads. An example of a typical conversation is:

> A: Eh, dinner eat what?
> B: Dunno, you say *leh?*
> A: I also *chin chye.* Go Esplanade, want or not?
> B: Boleh.

What the conversation means:

> A: What shall we have for dinner?
> B: I'm undecided. What would you like?
> A: I'm easy. Shall we go to the Esplanade?
> B: Sure.

In the example, it is clear that Singlish and Manglish (quite often similar) replace much of the standard English vocabulary with local words. The linguistic borrowings are seen in the use of the words "boleh," Malay for "okay," and "chin chye," Hokkien for "anything goes." The words "lah" and "leh" are often appended at the end of the sentence for emphasis. Furthermore, the disregard of standard English grammatical and syntax rules is obvious.

Singlish and Manglish are often used as a source of humor. One of Singapore's most successful local television sitcoms, *Phua Chu Kang,* features a Singlish-spouting renovation contractor whose favorite line is "Don't play-play!" which he pronounces as "Don't pray pray!" The phase, which means "Don't mess around with me," is widely imitated by young Singaporeans and Malaysians. Manglish is also used in local literature, film, and even music to inject a distinctive Singaporean and Malaysian flavor to these arts. There are even dictionaries such as *The Coxford Singlish Dictionary* and online Manglish dictionaries to help those unfamiliar with these local Englishes.[1]

The deliberate use of Singlish and English in locals' day-to-day life is often regarded as humorous. The governments, however, do not see things as light-heartedly. For them, the widespread use of Singlish and Manglish signifies the declining local standards of English. There are both proponents and opponents of colloquial English. Proponents point to these English variants as critical components of national culture that help create a sense of belonging among citizens. There are, however, strong opponents among government officials, educators, and language professionals who regard Singlish and Manglish merely as poor or deficient forms of English. They are seen as a variety of English that puts Singaporeans and Malaysians at a disadvantage because they are not internationally intelligible. Since 2000, the Singapore government has launched the "Speak Good English Movement" to encourage Singaporeans "to speak grammatically correct English that is universally understood." In Malaysia, since 2001, a local newspaper, *The Star,* has embarked on a campaign dubbed "Mind Our English" to promote the "correct use of English." Despite these efforts, many Singaporeans and Malaysians persist in speaking their colloquial Englishes, especially in informal contexts. The younger and better-educated generations have become proficient in code-switching, that is, using standard English in formal and business setting while falling back on Singlish or Manglish when speaking to friends and family.

MANAGING MULTICULTURALISM

Often described as melting pots of diverse cultures, Singapore and Malaysia are indeed home to a range of ethnic groups and their ways of life. The groups are free to practice their customs and culture relatively freely. Both the Singapore and the Malaysian governments have attributed their achievements in the past few decades to the successful management of multiculturalism and multiracialism, touted as two key social pillars. Undercurrents of tension, however, are present. In both Singapore and Malaysia, ethnicity and ethnic loyalties are constant concerns. Communalism—loyalty and commitment to one's own ethnic group and its interest—was a major factor that drove a wedge between Singapore and Malaysia during the 1950s and 1960s. It is still a dominant force in Malaysian society, with the issue of Malays' political and cultural dominance of Malaysia being particularly pertinent. In Malaysia, scholars and commentators have pointed to the presence of rival ethnic interests or nationalisms in Malaysian society, involving the Malays, the dominant community; indigenous communities; and other ethnic groups, such the Chinese and the Indians.[2] Efforts at creating a national identity and sentiment are made difficult by ethnic divisions.

Several events in recent years serve as prominent reminders of the fragility of ethnic relations that underlie Malaysia's pluralism. Among the non-Malays, there has been seething unease about the dominance of Malays in Malaysian society and the discriminatory practices against minority groups. At a 2005 United Malays National Organization youth assembly, the UMNO Youth chief, who was also a cabinet minister, brandished the *kris* (a traditional Malay dagger), which had been proposed that year in the Assembly as a symbol of Malay culture. He repeated this behavior the following year, and he and several UMNO delegates made remarks that commentators saw as constituting a threat to those who opposed special rights for Malays as set out in the Constitution. Although he apologized for his provocative act, many non-Malay Malaysians felt uneasy.

The issue of special Malay rights and Malay dominance in Malaysia has come to a head in the past few years. In 2007, more than 10,000 Indians staged a major antigovernment protest over the marginalization of their group as a result of government affirmative action policies that favor ethnic Malays. Many Indians complained about a lack of educational and business opportunities. More recently, in 2008, a UMNO member commented during a by-election campaign that the Chinese in Malaysia were mostly squatters who had no right to equal treatment with the Malays, who are considered Malaysia's natives. These comments drew fire from Malaysia's Chinese and Indian populations and brought the issue of race to the surface. Although the politician was suspended from the party, he refused to apologize, maintaining that his statement was a "historical fact."

These underlying pressures are motivating political and social change in Malaysia. In 2008, the ruling Barisan Nasional (BN) coalition of three ethnically-based political parties—UMNO, MCA (Malaysian Chinese Association), and MIC (Malaysian Indian Congress)—suffered a major political defeat. Although the coalition won the elections, it failed to win a two-thirds majority for the first time since 1969, losing five state assemblies to the opposition. It has been argued that the BN's poor performance was a manifestation of the electorate's dissatisfaction over racial discrimination. At the same time, these movements suggest that major change is coming to Malaysian society, which historically has been characterized by Malay domination of politics, government, society, and culture.

In Singapore, ethnicity is a public issue and race relations are highly managed. The government emphasizes the need to maintain racial harmony to ensure a stable environment for economic growth and to prevent a recurrence of the death and destruction that resulted from racially motivated riots in the 1950s and 1960s. Race is managed through a variety of policies. An example is the existence of ethnic quotas for all public housing, which are set according to the current proportion of each ethnic group in Singapore's population. In every new estate, there is a deliberate policy of maintaining an appropriate proportional distribution of units among the three major ethnic groups in Singapore: Chinese, Malays, and Indians. The government argues that the policy is in place to prevent the emergence of ethnic enclaves that might lead to disintegration of the society.

Although the Malays are seen as being dominant in Malaysia, there are claims that they are discriminated against in Singapore. The fear that Malay loyalty to Singapore may supersede national patriotism is a recurring one for the government. A statement made in 1999 by the former Singapore prime minister Lee Kuan Yew, who was by then the senior minister, highlighted this issue. At a forum, in response to a question about whether instinctive ethnic bonds could be overcome by national loyalty, Lee acknowledged that, while it was possible, it would take a long time and happen selectively. He then proceeded to give an example:

If, for instance, you put in a Malay officer who's very religious and who has family ties in Malaysia in charge of a machine gun unit, that's a very tricky business. We've got to know his background. I'm saying these things because they are real, and if I don't think that, and I think even if today the Prime Minister doesn't think carefully about this, we could have a tragedy.[3]

Lee's remarks raised a controversy among the local Malay community, who felt slighted. Many felt that the remarks affirmed a longheld perception that the deliberate moves to not place Malays in sensitive positions in the armed forces, the government, and the civil service were essentially discriminatory and that these policies reinforced the relegation of the Malays to the political, socioeconomic, and educational margins of Singapore society. Some scholars have suggested that the Singapore government's minimalist approach to the Malay community—stressing meritocracy and equal rights for all ethnic groups, instead of granting them special privileges, as in Malaysia—does not improve the life of the Malay community in Singapore.[4]

New Media and Society

In the past decade, the Singapore and Malaysia governments have been assertive in developing their technological infrastructures. The Malaysian Multimedia Super Corridor (MSC) project is an initiative focused on developing the Malaysian global information and communication technology (ICT) industry in its bid to achieve developed-nation status by 2020. Singapore's latest master plan for information technology development is Intelligent Nation 2015 (iN2015), which has as its goal to make Singapore number one in the world in harnessing information and communications to add value to the economy and society. These advances in infrastructure have led to a great increase in the number of Singaporeans and Malaysians using new media, specifically the Internet.

Many young Singaporeans and Malaysians are among the most computer and Internet savvy in the world. In 2007, 74 percent of Singapore's households had access to the Internet,[5] while Malaysia's broadband Internet penetration rate was 14.4 percent.[6] Internet cafés are a common sight in Singapore and in many of Malaysia's cities. Wireless connection is also widely available in many cafés, restaurants and other public places. The Internet has become a new source of information and entertainment. Singaporeans and Malaysians are able to access a wider range of information and entertainment beyond their normal sources of press, magazines, television, and movies, which are all, to a certain extent, subject to government censorship or control. Many organizations, including governmental departments, also make use of the Internet to disseminate news and information through their dedicated Web sites.

In addition, the Internet has become a way for Singaporeans and Malaysians to interact and discuss politically sensitive issues and all other topics. The Internet is particularly significant as an alternative medium in Singapore and Malaysia, where the mainstream media are largely pro-government because they are controlled by the government. Furthermore, popular participation or discussion in the mainstream press and on broadcasting networks is limited by a host of laws and censorship controls. The Internet is thus one of the few public media that can operate with relative freedom and few restrictions. In Malaysia, for example, the online newspaper Malaysiakini.com offers alternative news and views on Malaysian issues that are often not available from the mainstream press.

In addition to news and information, the Internet has also created an enlarged social community. Singaporeans and Malaysians are not just dependent on the World Wide Web for news and information; the young especially also build their social life around the Internet. Facebook, MySpace, and Friendster are among the most popular social networking sites that the youngsters use on a regular basis. The amount of user-generated content in the form of blogs (online Web journals), podcasts, and digital video has skyrocketed in the past few years. The content ranges from the humorous or satirical to the political, or just simply the social. Blogs, in particular, have emerged as a significant online medium with a major impact on Singapore and Malaysian societies. Malaysia has a number of active political bloggers such as Lim Kit Siang and Jeffrey Ooi, who use their blogs to rally readers to their particular brand of opposition politics. In Singapore, politics has less of a presence in the blogosphere, but the Internet has nonetheless become an arena for critiquing the government, albeit with humor, in blogs such as Mrbrown.com and TalkingCock.com.

RELATIONS BETWEEN SINGAPORE AND MALAYSIA

Singapore and Malaysia entered the 21st century on confident footings. Both countries have developed economies and stable political and administrative infrastructures and enjoy relative peace and stability. Both countries are partners in regional organizations, such as ASEAN (Association of Southeast Asian Nations), among others. Although the painful experience of merger and separation has dulled with time, their relatively peaceful bilateral relations are still touchy at times. Some long-running squabbles continue over territorial disputes, water supply and payment, and the Malaysian Railway land holdings in Singapore. One of the most prominent territorial disputes between the two countries is over a small outlying island, Pedra Branca, which is known as Pulau Batu Puteh to Malaysians. For almost 30 years, both countries have failed to resolve the issue of sovereignty over the island, on which is the Horsburgh Lighthouse, built in the 1840s, and other maritime features nearby. The matter was brought to the International Court of Justice (ICJ) for resolution. On May 23, 2008, the ICJ ruled that Pedra Branca is under Singapore's sovereignty, while the nearby Middle Rocks remain Malaysian territory. In 1996, Singapore's former prime minister Lee Kuan Yew broached the topic of a re-merger between Singapore and Malaysia. The idea sparked widespread controversy. Many Singaporeans and Malaysians were against it for different reasons, the most important of which is that members of the older generation still vividly remembered the unhappy past.

Politically, strong undercurrents of rivalry between Singapore and Malaysia remain. Much of the rivalry can be attributed to the political animosities during the brief period of merger (1963–1965). The subsequent separation has given both countries a chip on the shoulder. Singapore wants to prove that it can survive without Malaysia, while the latter seeks to prove that it is better off without Singapore, long seen as a political thorn in its side. Some Malaysian commentators see Singapore as a "pimple that won't burst" on the face of Malaysia. Together with Indonesia, Malaysia constantly reminds Singapore of its small size and notes that Malaysia is Singapore's *abang*, big brother. Singapore, on the other hand, refuses to acknowledge that its status is relative to its size. Since independence in 1965, Singapore has developed rapidly into a modern and industrialized country. It is one of the four economic mini-dragons of Asia, together with South Korea, Taiwan, and Hong Kong. Some have suggested that Malaysia is envious of Singapore's economic success.

Under Prime Minister Mahathir Mohammad, Malaysia has also embarked on a path of phenomenal growth. With that has come a patriotic sense of achievement. "*Malaysia boleh!*" meaning "Malaysia can do it," was a slogan that accompanied the government's aspiration of turning Malaysia into a developed country by the year 2020. A project that highlights the *Malaysia boleh* spirit is the *Malaysian Book of Records,* which is the Malaysian equivalent to the *Guinness Book of World Records* and which documents all the records and achievements of extraordinary feats by Malaysians. Some have labeled the project as simply a way to "show off," with some records bordering on the trivial and the ridiculous, such as that for the longest distance swum (50 meters) by a toddler (2 years 6 months) and that for the greatest number of heads shampooed in one day at a shopping mall (1,068).

Although Singapore and Malaysia are two separate and independent political entities, they share the same historical and cultural genesis. Returning to the siblings analogy in Chapter 1, we can see Singapore and Malaysia as two siblings in the same family, each with its own personality and temperament. As each one comes into its own, disputes and squabbles are inevitable. Ultimately, however, the cultural bond is hard to sever.

NOTES

1. See for example, the *Coxford Singlish Dictionary,* http://www.talkingcock.com/html/lexec.php?lexicon=lexicon&op=LexPKL; and *Urban Dictionary,* http://www.urbandictionary.com/define.php?term=manglish.

2. Cheah Boon Kheng (ed.), *The Challenge of Ethnicity: Building a Nation in Malaysia* (Singapore: Cavendish Academic, 2004).

3. Ahmad Osman, "Malay-Muslims Want Dialogue with SM," *Straits Times,* September 29, 1999.

4. See, for example, Lily Zubaidah Rahim, *The Singapore Dilemma: The Political and Educational Marginality of the Malay Community* (Kuala Lumpur: Oxford University Press, 1998).

5. Infocom Development Authority, Singapore. *IDA's annual survey on Infocomm usage in households and by individuals for 2007,* www.ida.gov.sg/doc/Publications/Publications_Level2/20061205092557/ASInfocommUsageHseholds07.pdf.

6. Malaysian Communications and Multimedia Commission, *Penetration Rate of the Communications and Multimedia Industry,* http://www.skmm.gov.my/facts_fig ures/stats/index.asp.

SUGGESTED READINGS

Cheah, Boon Kheng (ed.). *The Challenge of Ethnicity: Building a Nation in Malaysia.* Singapore: Cavendish Academic, 2004.

Chng, Huang Hoon. "'You See Me No Up': Is Singlish a Problem?," *Language Problems and Language Planning* 27, no. 1 (2003): 45–62.

Lily Zubaidah Rahim. *The Singapore Dilemma: The Political and Educational Marginality of the Malay Community.* Kuala Lumpur: Oxford University Press, 1998.

Vasil, Raj K. *Asianising Singapore: The PAP's Management of Ethnicity,* Singapore: Heinemann Asia, 1995.

Bibliography

Achievements Off the Beaten Track: Stories of Singapore Sports Veterans. Singapore: Candid Creation, 2005.

Ackerman, Susan, and Raymond Lee. *Heaven in Transition: Non-Muslim Religious Innovation and Ethnic Identity in Malaysia.* Honolulu: University of Hawaii Press, 1988.

Ahmad Osman. "Malay-Muslims Want Dialogue with SM." *The Straits Times,* September 29, 1999.

Andaya, Barbara Watson, and Leonard Andaya. *A History of Malaysia* (2nd ed.). Honolulu: University of Hawaii Press, 2001.

Ang, Ien, and Jon Stratton. "The Singapore Way of Multiculturalism: Western Concepts/Asian Cultures." *Sojourn* 10, no.1 (1995).

Asmah Haji Oman (ed.). *The Encyclopedia of Malaysia: Languages and Literature.* Singapore: Editions Didier Millet, 2004.

Baker, Jim. *Crossroads: A Popular History of Malaysia and Singapore* (2nd ed.). Singapore: Marshall Cavendish International, 2008.

Benjamin, Geoffrey, and Cynthia Chou (eds). *Tribal Communities in the Malay World: Historical, Cultural and Sociological Perspectives.* Singapore: Institute of Southeast Asian Studies, 2002.

Bird, Isabella. *The Golden Chersonese and the Way Thither.* Kuala Lumpur: Oxford University Press, 1967.

Brown, C. C. (trans.). *Sejarah Melayu, or Malay Annals.* Kuala Lumpur: Oxford University Press, 1970.

Chan, Margaret. *Margaret Chan's Foodstops.* Singapore: Landmark Books, 1992.

Cheah, Boon Kheng (ed.). *The Challenge of Ethnicity: Building a Nation in Malaysia.* Singapore: Cavendish Academic, 2004.

Chen, May Yee. *The Royal Selangor Story: Born and Bred in Pewter Dust.* Kuala Lumpur: Archipelago Press, 2003.

Chen, Voon Fee. *The Encyclopedia of Malaysia: Architecture.* Singapore: Archipelago Press, 1998.

Chin, Peng. *My Side of History, as Told to Ian Ward and Norma O. Miraflor.* Singapore: Media Masters, 2003.

Chng, Huang Hoon. "'You See Me No Up': Is Singlish a Problem?" *Language Problems and Language Planning* 27, no. 1 (2003): 45–62.

Clammer, John. *Singapore: Ideology, Society, Culture.* Singapore: Chopmen, 1985.

Costumes Through Time. Singapore: National Heritage Board and Fashion Design Society, 1993.

De Cotta, Ian. *The Singapore Grand Prix: 50 Years In The Making.* Singapore: MediaCorp, 2008.

Devi, Uma, et al. *Singapore's 100 Historic Places.* Singapore: Archipelago Press in association with National Heritage Board, 2002.

Djamour, Judith. *Malay Kinship and Marriage in Singapore.* London: Athlone Press, 1965.

Farish A. Noor. *From Majapahit to Putrajaya: Searching for Another Malaysia.* Kuala Lumpur: Silverfish, 2005.

Farish A. Noor. *Spirit of Wood: The Art of Malay Woodcarving.* Hong Kong: Periplus, 2003.

Fealy, Greg, and Virginia Hooker (eds.). *Voices of Islam in Southeast Asia: A Contemporary Sourcebook.* Singapore: Institute of Southeast Asia Studies, 2006.

Freedman, Maurice. *The Chinese in South-East Asia: A Longer View.* London: China Society, 1965.

Funston, John (ed.). *Government and Politics in Southeast Asia.* Singapore: Institute of Southeast Asia Studies, 2001.

Garrett, Valery M. *Traditional Chinese Clothing.* Hong Kong: Oxford University Press, 1987.

Ghulam-Sarwar Yousof. *The Encyclopedia of Malaysia: Performing Arts.* Singapore: Archipelago Press, 1998.

Ghulam-Sarwar Yousof. "Traditional Theatre in Southeast Asia." *Performing Arts* 2 (July 1985).

Gibbs, Philip. *Building a Malay House.* Singapore: Oxford University Press, 1987.

Gonzales, Joseph. *Choreography: A Malaysian Perspective.* Kuala Lumpur: Akademi Seni Kebangsaan, 2004.

Haji Abdul Ghani Haji Bujang et al. *Visual Arts in ASEAN: Continuity and Change.* Kuala Lumpur: ASEAN Committee on Culture and Information, 2001.

Hall, D. G. E. *A History of Southeast Asia.* London: Macmillan, 1968.

Hasnah Haji Ibrahim (ed.). *Anthology of ASEAN Literatures, Malaysia: Indigenous Traditions.* Kuala Lumpur: ASEAN Committee on Culture and Information, 1985.

Hutton, Wendy. *Singapore Food.* Singapore: Marshall Cavendish, 2007.

Ismail Hamid. *The Malay Islamic Hikayat.* Selangnor: Penerbit Universiti Kebangsaan Malaysia, 1983.

Kong, Lily. *Singapore Hawker Centres: People, Places, Food.* Singapore: National Environment Agency, 2007.

Kwok, Kian Chow. *Channels and Confluences: A History of Singapore Art.* Singapore: Singapore Art Museum, 1996.

Lasimbang, Rita, and Stella Moo-Tan. *An Introduction to the Traditional Costumes of Sabah.* Kota Kinabalu: Natural History Publications in association with Department of Sabah Museum, 1997.

Lau, Albert. *A Moment of Anguish.* Singapore: Oxford University Press, 1998.

Lee, Kip Lin. *The Singapore House 1819–1942.* Singapore: Times Editions [for] Preservation of Monuments Board, 1988.

Leiter, Samuel L. (ed.). *Encyclopedia of Asian Theatre, Vol. 1.* Westport, CT: Greenwood Press, 2007.

Leong, Gregory. *Festivals of Malaysia.* Selangor: Pelanduk Publications, 1992.

Lily Zubaidah Rahim. *The Singapore Dilemma: The Political and Educational Marginality of the Malay Community.* Kuala Lumpur: Oxford University Press, 1998.

Lip, Evelyn. *Chinese Temples and Deities.* Singapore: Times Books International, 1986.

Lockard, Craig. *Dance of Life: Popular Music and Politics in Southeast Asia.* Honolulu: University of Hawaii Press, 1998.

Loong, May Lin. *On Television on Singapore.* Singapore: Singapore Broadcasting Corporation, 1988.

Lu, Sylvia Fraser. *Handwoven Textiles of Southeast Asia.* Singapore: Oxford University Press, 1989.

Lu, Sylvia Fraser. *Silverware of Southeast Asia.* Singapore: Oxford University Press, 1989.

Mahathir Mohammad. *The Way Forward.* Working paper presented at the Malaysian Business Council, Kuala Lumpur, 1991, http:www.pmo.gov.my/?menu=page&page=1904, accessed November 29, 2008.

Mandakini, Arora. *Small Steps, Giant Leaps: A History of AWARE and the Women's Movement in Singapore.* Singapore: Association of Women for Action and Research, 2007.

Matusky, Patricia, and Tan Sooi Beng. *The Music of Malaysia: The Classical, Folk and Syncretic Traditions.* Aldershot: Ashgate, 2004.

McDaniel, Drew O. *Broadcasting in the Malay World: Radio, Television and Video in Brunei, Indonesia, Malaysia and Singapore.* Norwood, NJ: Ablex, 1994.

McDougall, Colin. *Buddhism in Malaya.* Singapore: D. Moore, 1956.

Michell, George. *The Hindu Temple: An Introduction to Its Meaning and Forms.* London: Paul Elek, 1977.

Millet, Raphael. *Singapore Cinema.* Singapore: Editions Didier Millet, 2006.

Mohd Ismail Noor (ed.). *The Food of ASEAN.* Kuala Lumpur: ASEAN Committee on Culture and Information, 2000.

Mohd Najib Ahmad Dawa (ed.). *Susurmasa (Timelines)*. Malaysia: National Art Gallery, Malaysia, 2008.

Mohd Taib Osman. *An Introduction to the Development of Modern Malay Language and Literature*. Singapore: Times Books International, 1986.

Muliyadi Mahmood. *Modern Malaysian Art: From the Pioneering Era to the Pluralist Era (1930s–1990s)*. Kuala Lumpur: Utusan Publications and Distributors, 2007.

National Arts Council. *Literature in Singapore*. Singapore: National Arts Council, 2007.

"New Directions," *Straits Times,* April 27, 1991.

Ong, Y. D. *Buddhism in Singapore: A Short Narrative History*. Singapore: Skylark, 2005.

Pham, Duc Thanh (ed.). *Traditional Festivals of Asean*. Hanoi: ASEAN Committee on Culture and Information, 2003.

Powell, Robert. *Singapore Architecture*. Hong Kong: Periplus, 2004.

Raine, Nick, and Andy Raine. *Sabah. Sarawak: Land, People and Cultures*. Kuala Lumpur: S Abdul Majeed, 1995.

Redza, Piyadasa. "Modern Malaysian Art 1945–1991: A Historical Overview." In Caroline Turner (ed.), *Tradition and Change: Contemporary Art of Asia and the Pacific*. Queensland: University of Queensland Press, 1993.

Roziah Omar, and Azizah Hamzah (eds.). *Women in Malaysia: Breaking Boundaries*. Kuala Lumpur: Utusan Publications and Distributions, 2003.

Sandhu, Kernial Singh, and A. Mani (eds.). *Indian Communities in Southeast Asia*. Singapore: Institute of Southeast Asian Studies, 2006.

Sandhu, Kernial Singh, and Paul Wheatley (eds.). *Management of Success: The Moulding of Modern Singapore*. Singapore: Institute of Southeast Asian Studies, 1989.

Santos, Ramon P. (ed.). *The Music of ASEAN*. Brunei Darussalam: ASEAN Committee on Culture and Information, 1995.

Saw, Swee Hock. *The Population of Malaysia*. Singapore: Institute of Southeast Asian Studies, 2007.

Saw, Swee Hock. *The Population of Singapore*. Singapore: Institute of Southeast Asian Studies, 2007.

Sedyawati Edi (ed.). *The Theatre of ASEAN*. Brunei Darussalam: ASEAN Committee on Culture and Information, 2001.

Shahrum Yub. *The Keris and Other Short Weapons*. Kuala Lumpur: Museum Association of Malaysia, 1991.

Shennan, Margaret. *Out in the Midday Sun: The British in Malaya 1880–1960*. London: John Murray, 2000.

Sheppard, Mubin. *Living Crafts of Malaysia*. Singapore: Times Books International, 1978.

Short, Anthony. *The Communist Insurrection in Malaya 1948–1960*. London: Muller, 1975.

Sim, Katherine. *More Than a Pantun: Understanding Malay Verse*. Singapore: Times Books International, 1987.

Syed Ahmad Jamal (ed.). *The Encyclopedia of Malaysia, Vol. 14: Crafts and the Visual World.* Singapore: Editions Didier Millet, 2007.

Tan, Su-Lyn. *Lonely Planet World Food Malaysia and Singapore.* Footscray, Victoria, Australia: Lonely Planet, 2003.

Through the Decades: Malaysia's 50 Years of Sporting Glory. Selangor: E Publication in association with SEN Media, 2007.

Thumboo, Edwin, et al. *The Fiction of Singapore.* Singapore: Unipress, 1993.

Turnbull, Mary. *A History of Singapore 1819–1988* (2nd ed.). Singapore: Oxford University Press, 1997.

Van der Heide, William. *Malaysian Cinema, Asian Film.* Amsterdam: Amsterdam University Press, 2002.

Vasil, Raj K. *Asianising Singapore: The PAP's Management of Ethnicity.* Singapore: Heinemann Asia, 1995.

Vlatseas, S. *A History of Malaysian Architecture.* Singapore: Longman, 1990.

White, Timothy. "When Singapore Was Southeast Asia's Hollywood." *The Arts* 5 (December 1997).

Winstedt, Sir Richard. *A History of Malaya* (revised ed.). Singapore: Marican & Sons, 1962.

Winstedt, Sir Richard. *The Malay Magician* (revised ed.). London: Routledge, 1951.

Yea, Sallie. "On and Off the Ethnic Tourism Map in Southeast Asia: The Case of Iban Longhouse Tourism, Sarawak, Malaysia." *Tourism Geographies* 4, Issue 2 (May 2002).

Yeang, Ken. *The Architecture of Malaysia.* Amsterdam: Pepin Press, 1992.

Yeo, Song Nian. "Chinese Language Literature in Malaya and Singapore (1919–1942)." In Leo Suryadinata (ed.), *Chinese Adaptation and Diversity: Essays on Society and Literature in Indonesia, Malaysia and Singapore.* Singapore: Singapore University Press, 1993.

Zainal Abiddin Tinggal (ed.). *The Dances of ASEAN.* Brunei Darussalam: ASEAN Committee on Culture and Information, 1998.

Zakaria, Fareed. "Culture Is Destiny—A Conversation with Lee Kuan Yew." *Foreign Affairs* 73, no. 2 (March/April 1994).

Index

About the Authors

JAIME KOH, a former journalist and writer, has a deep interest in Asian history, culture, and politics. She has traveled widely across the region and has worked in Singapore and Australia. She is bilingual in English and Mandarin, speaks several dialects, and is a keen photographer. Jaime manages a research consultancy and is currently pursuing her doctorate at the National University of Singapore.

STEPHANIE HO, a former history teacher and museum educator, has a longstanding interest in the social and cultural history of Singapore and Malaysia. Her expertise in this field comes from practical experiences as well as academic study. She has a PhD in Public History from the University of Technology, Sydney (UTS). Stephanie is also a published author and illustrator of children's books. Her books *Samsui Girl* (2006) and *Wayang Girl* (2008) are inspired by Singapore's historical icons and seek to educate children about them in a fun and humorous manner.

WOODLAND HIGH SCHOOL
800 N. MOSELEY DRIVE
STOCKBRIDGE, GA 30281
(770) 389-2784